WHAT SHALL WE DO?

BY
LEO TOLSTOY

WHAT SHALL WE DO?

"And the people asked him, saying, What shall we do then?

"He answereth and said unto them, He that hath two coats, let him impart to him that hath none; and he that hath meat, let him do likewise." (Luke iii. 10, 11.)

"Lay not up for yourselves treasures upon earth, where moth and rust doth corrupt, and where thieves break through and steal:

"But lay up for yourselves treasures in heaven, where neither moth nor rust doth corrupt, and where thieves do not break through nor steal:

"For where your treasure is, there will your heart be also.

"The light of the body is the eye; if, therefore, thine eye be single, thy whole body shall be full of light.

"But if thine eye be evil, thy whole body shall be full of darkness. If, therefore, the light that is in thee be darkness, how great is your darkness?

"No man can serve two masters: for either he will hate the one, and love the other; or else he will hold to the one, and despise the other. Ye cannot serve God and mammon.

"Therefore I say unto you, Take no thought for your life, what ye shall eat, or what ye shall drink; nor yet for your body, what ye shall put on. Is not the life more than meat, and the body than raiment?" (Matt. vi. 19–25.)

"Therefore take no thought, saying, What shall we eat? or, What shall we drink? or, Wherewithal shall we be clothed?

"(For after all these things do the Gentiles seek): for your heavenly Father knoweth that ye have need of all these things.

"But seek ye first the kingdom of God, and his righteousness; and all these things shall be added unto you." (Matt. vi. 31–33.)

"For it is easier for a camel to go through a needle's eye, than for a rich man to enter into the kingdom of God." (Luke xviii. 25.)

CHAPTER I

After having passed the greater part of my life in the country, I came at length, in the year 1881, to reside in Moscow, where I was immediately struck with the extreme state of pauperism in that city. Though well acquainted with the privations of the poor in rural districts, I had not the faintest conception of their actual condition in towns.

In Moscow it is impossible to pass a street without meeting beggars of a peculiar kind, quite unlike those in the country, who go about there, as the saying is, "with a bag and the name of Christ."

The Moscow beggars neither carry a bag nor ask for alms. In most cases when they meet you, they try to catch your eye, and then act according to the expression of your face.

I know of one such, a bankrupt gentleman. He is an old man who advances slowly, limping painfully with each leg. When he meets you, he limps, and makes a bow. If you stop, he takes off his cap, ornamented with a cockade, bows again, and begs. If you do not stop, he pretends to be only lame, and continues limping along.

That is a specimen of a genuine Moscow beggar, an experienced one.

At first I did not know why such mendicants did not ask openly; but afterwards I learned why, without understanding the reason.

One day I saw a policeman push a ragged peasant swollen with dropsy, into a cab. I asked what he had been doing, and the policeman replied,—

"Begging."

"Is begging, then, forbidden?"

"So it seems," he answered. As the man was being driven away, I took another cab, and followed. I wished to find out whether begging was really forbidden, and if so, why? I could not at all understand how it was possible to forbid one man asking something from another; and, moreover, I had my doubts whether it could be illegal in a city where it flourished to such an extent.

I entered the police-station where the pauper had been taken, and asked an official armed with sword and pistol, and seated at a table, what he had been arrested for.

The man looked up at me sharply, and said, "What business is that of yours?"

However, feeling the necessity of some explanation, he added, "The authorities order such fellows to be arrested, so I suppose it is necessary."

I went away. The policeman who had brought the man was sitting in the window of the ante-room, studying his note-book. I said to him,—

"Is it really true that poor people are not allowed to ask for alms in Christ's name?"

The man started, as if waking up from a sleep, stared at me, then relapsed again into a state of stolid indifference, and, reseating himself on the window-sill, said,—

"The authorities require it, so you see it is necessary."

As he became again absorbed in his note-book, I went down the steps towards my cab.

"Well! have they locked him up?" asked the cabman. He had evidently become interested in the matter.

"They have," I answered. He shook his head.

"Is begging forbidden in Moscow, then?" I asked.

"I can't tell you," he said.

"But how can a man be locked up," I said, "for begging in the name of Christ?"

"Nowadays things have changed, and you see it is forbidden," he answered.

Since then, I have often seen policemen taking paupers to the police-station and thence to the work-house. Indeed, I once met a whole crowd of these poor creatures, about thirty, escorted before and behind by policemen. I asked what they had been doing.

"Begging," was the reply.

It appears that, according to law, begging is forbidden in Moscow, notwithstanding the great number of beggars one meets there in every street, notwithstanding the rows of them near the churches during service-time, and especially at funerals. But why are some caught and locked up, while others are let alone? This I have not been able to find out. Either there are lawful and unlawful beggars amongst them, or else there are so many that it is impossible to catch them all; or, perhaps, though some are taken up, others fill their places.

There is a great variety of such beggars in Moscow. There are those who live by begging. There are also entirely honest destitute people who have somehow chanced to reach Moscow and are really in extreme need.

Amongst the latter are men and women evidently from the country. I have often met these. Some of them, who had fallen ill and afterwards recovered and left the hospital, could now find no means, either of feeding themselves, or of getting away from Moscow; some of them, besides, had taken to drink (this was probably the case with the man with dropsy whom I met); some were in good health, but had been burned out of house and home, or else were very old, or were widowed or deserted women with children; and some others had sound health, and were quite capable of working.

These robust people especially interested me,—the more so, because, since my arrival in Moscow, I had contracted the habit of going to the Sparrow Hills for the sake of exercise, and working there with two peasants who sawed wood. These men were exactly like the beggars whom I often met in the streets. One, called Peter, was an ex-soldier from Kaluga; the other, Simon, was from Vladímir. They possessed nothing save the clothes on their backs: and they earned, by working very hard, from forty to forty-five kopeks (8d. to 9d.) a day; out of this they both put a little aside,—the Kaluga soldier, to buy a fur coat; the Vladímir peasant, to get money enough to return to his home in the country.

Meeting in the streets similar men, I was therefore particularly interested in them, and could not understand why some begged whilst others worked.

Whenever I met a beggar of this description, I used to ask him how it was that he had come to such a state. Once I met a strong, healthy-looking peasant who asked alms. I questioned him as to who he was, and whence he had come.

He told me he had come from Kaluga, in search of work. He had at first found some, such as sawing old timber into fire-wood; but after he and his companion had finished that job, though they had continually looked for it, they had not found any more work, his mate had left him, and he himself had passed a fortnight in the utmost need, and having sold all he had to get food, now had not enough even to buy the necessary tools for sawing.

I gave him money to get a saw, and told him where to go for work. I had previously arranged with Peter and Simon that they should accept a new fellow-worker, and find him a mate.

"Be sure you come! There is plenty of work to be done," I said on parting.

"You can reckon on me," he answered. "Do you think there is any pleasure in knocking about, begging, if I can work?"

The man solemnly promised that he would come; and he seemed honest, and really meaning to work.

Next day, on coming to my friends, Peter and Simon, I asked them whether the man had arrived. They said he had not; and, indeed, he never came at all. In this way I was frequently deceived.

I have also been deceived by those who said that they only wanted a little money to buy a ticket to return home, and whom I met in the streets again a few days later. Many of them I came to know well, and they knew me; though occasionally having forgotten me, they would repeat the same false tale; but sometimes they would turn away on recognizing me.

In this way I discovered, that, even in this class of men, there are many rogues.

Still, these poor rogues were also very much to be pitied: they were all ragged and hungry; they were of the sort who die of cold in the streets, or hang themselves to escape life, as the papers frequently tell us.

CHAPTER II

When I talked to my town friends about this pauperism which surrounded them, they always replied, "Oh! you have seen nothing yet! You should go to the Khitrof Market, and visit the lodging-houses there, if you want to see the genuine 'Golden Company.'"

One jovial friend of mine added, that the number of these paupers had so increased, that they already formed not a "Golden Company," but a "Golden Regiment."

My witty friend was right; but he would have been yet nearer the truth had he said that these men formed, in Moscow, not a company, nor a regiment, but a whole army,—an army, I should judge, of about fifty thousand.

The regular townspeople, when they spoke to me about the pauperism of the city, always seemed to feel a certain pleasure or pride in being able to give me such precise information.

I remember I noticed, when visiting London, that the citizens there seemed also to find a certain satisfaction in telling me about London destitution, as though it were something to be proud of.

However, wishing to inspect this poverty about which I had heard so much, I had turned my steps very often towards the Khitrof Market,—but on each occasion I felt a sensation of pain and shame. "Why should you go to look at the suffering of human beings whom you cannot help?" said one voice within me. "If you live here, and see all that is pleasant in town life, go and see also what is wretched," replied another.

And so, one cold, windy day in December, two years ago (1883), I went to the Khitrof Market, the centre of the town pauperism.

It was on a week-day, about four in the afternoon. While still a good distance off I noticed greater and greater numbers of men in strange clothes,—evidently not originally meant for them,—and in yet stranger foot-wear; men of a peculiar unhealthy complexion, and all apparently showing a remarkable indifference to everything that surrounded them.

Men in the strangest, most incongruous costumes sauntered along, evidently without the least thought as to how they might look in the eyes of others. They were all going in the same direction. Without asking the way, which was unknown to me, I followed them, and came to the Khitrof Market.

There I found women likewise in ragged capes, rough cloaks, jackets, boots, and goloshes. Perfectly free and easy in their manner, notwithstanding the grotesque monstrosity of their attire, these women, old and young, were sitting, bargaining, strolling about, and abusing one another.

Market-time having evidently passed, there were not many people there; and as most of them were going up-hill, through the market-place, and all in the same direction, I followed them.

The farther I went, the greater became the stream of people flowing into the one road. Having passed the market, and gone up the street, I found that I was following two women, one old, the other young. Both were clothed in some grey ragged stuff. They were talking, as they walked, about some kind of business.

Every expression was unfailingly accompanied by some obscene word. Neither was drunk, but each absorbed with her own affairs; and the passing men, and those about them, paid not the slightest attention to their language, which sounded so strange to me. It appeared to be the generally accepted manner of speech in those parts. On the left we passed some private night-lodging-houses, and some of the crowd entered these; others continued to ascend the hill towards a large corner house. The majority of the people walking along with me went into this house. Before it, people all of the same sort were standing and sitting, on the sidewalk and in the snow.

At the right of the entrance were women; at the left, men. I passed by the men: I passed by the women (there were several hundreds in all), and stopped where the crowd ceased.

This building was the "Liapin free night-lodging-house" ("doss-house"). The crowd was composed of night-lodgers, waiting to be let in. At five o'clock in the evening this house is opened and the crowd admitted. Hither came almost all the people whom I followed.

I remained standing where the file of men ended. Those nearest stared at me till I had to look at them. The remnants of garments covering their bodies were very various; but the one expression of the eyes of all alike seemed to be, "Why are you, a man from another world, stopping here with us? Who are you? Are you a self-satisfied man of wealth, desiring to be gladdened by the sight of our need, to divert yourself in your idleness, and to mock at us? or are you that which does not and can not exist,—a man who pities us?"

On all their faces the same question was written. Each would look at me, meet my eyes, and turn away again.

I wanted to speak to some of them, but for a long time I could not summon up courage. However, eventually our mutual exchange of glances introduced us to each other; and we felt that, however widely separated might be our social positions in life, we were still fellow-men, and so we ceased to be afraid of one another.

Next to me stood a peasant with a swollen face and red beard, in a ragged jacket, with worn-out goloshes on his naked feet, though there were eight degrees of frost. For the third or fourth time our eyes met; and I felt so drawn to him that I was no longer ashamed to address him (to have refrained from doing so would have been the only real shame), and I asked him where he came from.

He answered eagerly, while a crowd began to collect round us, that he had come from Smolensk in search of work, to be able to buy bread and pay his taxes.

"There is no work to be had nowadays," he said: "the soldiers have got hold of it all. So here am I knocking about; and God is my witness, I have not had any thing to eat for two days."

He said this shyly, with an attempt at a smile. A seller of warm drinks, an old soldier, was standing near. I called him, and made him pour out a glass. The peasant took the warm vessel in his hands, and, before drinking, warmed them against the glass, trying not to lose any of the precious heat; and whilst doing this he related to me his story.

The adventures of these people, or at least the stories which they tell, are almost always the same: He had had a little work; then it had ceased: and here, in the night-lodging-house, his purse, containing his money and passport, had been stolen from him. Now he could not leave Moscow.

He told me that during the day he warmed himself in public-houses, eating any stale crust of bread which might be given him. His night's lodging here in Liapin's house cost him nothing.

He was only waiting for the round of the police-sergeant to lock him up for being without his passport, when he would be sent on foot, with a party of men similarly situated, to the place of his birth.

"They say the inspection will take place on Thursday, when I shall be taken up; so I must try and keep on until then." (The prison and his compulsory journey appeared to him as the "promised land.") While he was speaking, two or three men in the crowd said they were also in exactly the same situation.

A thin, pale youth, with a long nose, only a shirt upon his back, and that torn about the shoulders, and a tattered cap on his head, edged his way to me through the crowd. He was shivering violently all the time, but tried, as he caught my eye, to smile scornfully at the peasant's conversation, thinking thus to show his superiority.

I offered him some drink.

He warmed his hands on the tumbler as the other had done; but just as he began to speak, he was shouldered aside by a big, black, hook-nosed, bare-headed fellow, in a thin shirt and waistcoat, who also asked for some drink.

Then a tall old man, with a thin beard, in an overcoat fastened round the waist with a cord, and in bark shoes, had some. He was drunk.

Then came a little man, with a swollen face and wet eyes, in a coarse brown jacket, with his knees protruding through his torn trousers and knocking against each other with cold. He shivered so that he could not hold the glass, and spilled the contents over his clothes: the others began to abuse him, but he only grinned miserably, and shivered.

After him came an ugly, deformed man in rags, and with bare feet. Then an individual of the officer type; another belonging to the church class; then a strange-looking being without a nose,—all of them hungry, cold, suppliant, and humble,—crowded round me, and stretched out their hands for the glass; but the drink was exhausted. Then one man asked for money: I gave him some. A second and a third followed, till the whole crowd pressed on me. In the general confusion the gatekeeper of the neighbouring house shouted to the crowd to clear the pavement before his house, and the people submissively obeyed.

Some of them undertook to control the tumult, and took me under their protection. They attempted to drag me out of the crush. But the crowd that formerly had lined the pavement in a long file, had now become condensed about me. Every one looked at me and begged; and it seemed as if each face were more pitiful, harassed, and degraded than the other. I distributed all the money I had,—only about twenty rubles,—and entered the lodging-house with the crowd. The house was an enormous one, and consisted of four parts. In the upper storeys were the men's rooms; on the ground-floor the women's. I went first into the women's dormitory,—a large room, filled with beds resembling the berths in a third-class railway-carriage. They were arranged in two tiers, one above the other.

Strange-looking women in ragged dresses, without jackets, old and young, kept coming in and occupying places, some below, others climbing above. Some of the elder ones crossed themselves, pronouncing the name of the founder of the refuge. Some laughed and swore.

I went up-stairs. There, in a similar way, the men had taken their places. Amongst them I recognized one of those to whom I had given money. On seeing him I suddenly felt horribly ashamed, and made haste to leave.

With a sense of having committed some crime, I returned home. There I entered along the carpeted steps into the rug-covered hall, and, having taken off my fur coat, sat down to a meal of five courses, served by two footmen in livery, with white ties and white gloves. A scene of the past came suddenly before me. Thirty years ago I saw a man's head cut off under the guillotine in Paris before a crowd of thousands of spectators. I was aware that the man had been a great criminal: I was acquainted with all the arguments in justification of capital punishment for such offences. I saw this execution carried out deliberately: but at the moment that the head and body were severed from each other by the keen blade, I gasped, and realized in every fibre of my being, that all the arguments which I had hitherto heard in favour of capital punishment were wickedly false; that, no matter how many might agree that it was a lawful act, it was literally murder; whatever other title men might give it, they thus had virtually committed murder, that worst of all crimes: and there was I, both by my silence and my non-interference, an aider, an abetter, and participator in the sin.

Similar convictions were again forced upon me when I now beheld the misery, cold, hunger, and humiliation of thousands of my fellow-men. I realized not only with my brain, but in every pulse of my soul, that, whilst there were thousands of such sufferers in Moscow, I, with tens of thousands of others, daily filled myself to repletion with luxurious dainties of every description, took the tenderest care of my horses, and clothed my very floors with velvet carpets!

Whatever the wise and learned of the world might say about it, however unalterable the course of life might seem to be, the same evil was continually being enacted, and I, by my own personal habits of luxury, was a promoter of that evil.

The difference between the two cases was only this: that in the first, all I could have done would have been to shout out to the murderers standing near the guillotine, who were accomplishing the deed, that they were committing a murder, and by every means to try to hinder them,—while, of course, knowing that my interference would be in vain. Whereas, in this second case, I might have given away, not only the drink and the small sum of money I had with me, but also the coat from off my shoulders, and all that I possessed at home. Yet I had not done so, and therefore felt, and feel, and can never cease to feel, that I myself am a partaker in a crime which is continually being committed, so long as I have superfluous food whilst others have none, so long as I have two coats whilst there exists one man without any.

CHAPTER III

On the same evening that I returned from Liapin's house, I imparted my impressions to a friend: and he, a resident of the town, began to explain to me, not without a certain satisfaction, that this was the most natural state of things in a town; that it was only owing to my provincialism that I found anything remarkable in it; and that it had always been, and always would be so, such being one of the inevitable conditions of civilization. In London it was yet worse, etc., etc., therefore there could be nothing wrong about it, and there was nothing to be disturbed or troubled about.

I began to argue with my friend, but with such warmth and so angrily, that my wife rushed in from the adjoining room to ask what had happened. It appeared that, without being aware of it, I had shouted out in an agonized voice, gesticulating wildly, "We should not go on living in this way! we must not live so! we have no right!" I was rebuked for my unnecessary excitement; I was told that I could not talk quietly upon any question, that I was irritable; and it was pointed out to me that the existence of such misery as I had witnessed was in no way a reason for embittering the life of my home-circle.

I felt that this was perfectly just, and held my tongue; but in the depth of my soul I knew that I was right, and I could not quiet my conscience.

The town life, which had previously seemed alien and strange to me, now became so hateful that all the indulgencies of a luxurious existence, in which I had formerly delighted, began to torment me.

However much I tried to find some kind of excuse for my mode of life, I could not contemplate without irritation either my own or other people's drawing-rooms, nor a clean, richly served dinner-table, nor a carriage with well-fed coachman and horses, nor the shops, theatres, and entertainments. I could not help seeing, in contrast to all this, those hungry, shivering, and degraded inhabitants of the night-lodging-house. I could never free myself from the thought that these conditions were inseparable—that the one proceeded from the other. I remember that the sense of culpability which I had felt from the first moment never left me; but with this feeling another soon mingled, which lessened the first.

When I talked to my intimate friends and acquaintances about my impressions in Liapin's house, they all answered in the same way, and expressed besides their appreciation of my kindness and tender-heartedness, and gave me to understand that the sight had impressed me so because I, Leo Tolstoy, was kind-hearted and good. And I willingly allowed myself to believe this.

The natural consequence of this was, that the first keen sense of self-reproach and shame became blunted, and was replaced by a sense of satisfaction at my own virtue, and a desire to make it known to others. "It is, in truth," I said to myself, "probably not my connection with a luxurious life which is at fault, but the unavoidable circumstances of existence. Therefore a change in my particular life would not alter the evil I had seen."

In changing my own life, I thought, I should only render myself and those nearest and dearest to me miserable, whilst the other misery would remain; therefore my object should be, not to alter my own way of living, as I had at first imagined, but to try as much as was in my power to *ameliorate* the position of those unfortunate ones who had excited my compassion. The whole matter, I reasoned, lies in the fact that I, being an extremely kind and good man, wish to do good to my fellow-men.

So I began to arrange a plan of philanthropic activity in which I might exhibit all my virtues. I must, however, remark here, that, while planning this charitable effort, in the depth of my heart I felt that I was not doing the right thing; but, as too often happens, reason and imagination stifled the voice of conscience.

About this time the census was being taken, and this seemed to me a good opportunity for instituting that charitable organization in which I wanted to shine.

I was acquainted with many philanthropic institutions and societies already existing in Moscow, but all their activity seemed to me both insignificant and wrongly directed in comparison with what I myself wished to do.

This was what I invented to excite sympathy amongst the rich for the poor: I began to collect money, and to enlist men who wished to help in the work, and who would, in company with the census officers, visit all the nests of pauperism, entering into relations with the poor, finding out the details of their needs, aiding them with money and work, sending them out of Moscow, placing their children in schools, and their old men and women in homes and houses of refuge.

I thought, moreover, that from those who undertook this work a permanent society could be formed, which, by dividing between its members the various districts of Moscow, could take care that new cases of want and misery should be averted, and so by degrees pauperism might be stifled at its very beginning, not so much by cure, as by prevention.

Already I saw in the future the entire disappearance of begging and poverty, I having been the means of its accomplishment. Then we who were rich could go on living in all our luxury as before, dwelling in fine houses, eating dinners of five courses, driving in our carriages to theatres and entertainments, no longer being harassed by such sights as I had witnessed at Liapin's house.

Having invented this plan, I wrote an article about it; and, before even giving it to the printers, I went to those acquaintances from whom I hoped to obtain co-operation, and expounded to all whom I visited that day (chiefly the rich) the ideas I afterwards published in my article.

I proposed to profit by the census in order to study the state of pauperism in Moscow, and to help exterminate it by personal effort and money, after which we might all with a quiet conscience enjoy our usual pleasures. Everyone listened to me attentively and seriously; but, in every case, I remarked that the moment my hearers came to understand what I was driving at, they seemed to become uncomfortable and somewhat embarrassed. It was principally, I feel sure, on my own account; because they considered all that I said to be folly. It seemed as though some outside motive compelled my listeners to agree for the moment with my foolishness.—"Oh, yes! Certainly. It would be delightful," they said: "of course it is impossible not to sympathize with you. Your idea is splendid. I myself have had the same; but … people here are so indifferent, that it is hardly reasonable to expect a great success. However, as far as I am concerned, I am, of course, ready to share in the enterprise."

Similar answers I received from all. They consented, as it appeared to me, not because they were persuaded by my arguments, nor yet in compliance with their own desire, but because of some exterior reason which rendered it impossible for them to refuse.

I remarked this partly because none of those who promised me their help in the form of money, defined the sum they meant to give; so that I had to name the amount by asking, "May I count upon you for twenty-five, or one hundred, or two hundred, or three hundred, rubles?" And not one of them paid the money. I draw attention to this fact, because, when people are going to pay for what they are anxious to have, they are generally in haste to give it. If it is to secure a box to see Sarah Bernhardt, the money is immediately produced; here, however, of all who agreed to give, and expressed their sympathy, not one produced the amount, but merely silently acquiesced in the sum I happened to name.

In the last house I visited that day there was a large party. The mistress of the house had for some years been employed in works of charity. Several carriages were waiting at the door. Footmen in expensive liveries were seated in the hall. In the spacious drawing-room, ladies, old and young, wearing rich dresses and ornaments, were talking to some young men, and dressing up small dolls, intended for a lottery in aid of the poor.

The sight of this drawing-room and of the people assembled there struck me very painfully. For not only was their property worth several million rubles; not only would the interest on the capital spent here on dresses, laces, bronzes, jewels, carriages, horses, liveries, footmen, exceed a hundred times the value of these ladies' work,—but even the expenses caused by this very party of ladies and gentlemen, the gloves, the linen, candles, tea, sugar, cakes, all this represented a sum a hundred times greater than the value of the work done.

I saw all this, and therefore might have understood that here, at all events, I should not find sympathy with my plan, but I had come in order to give a proposal, and, however painful it was, I said what I wished to say, repeating almost the words of my article.

One lady present offered me some money, adding that, owing to her sensibilities, she did not feel strong enough to visit the poor herself, but that she would give help in this form. How much money, and when she would give it, she did not say. Another lady and a young man offered their services in visiting the poor, but I did not profit by their offer. The principal person I addressed told me that it would be impossible to do much, because the means were not forthcoming. The means were scarce, because all the rich men in Moscow who were known and could be counted upon had already given all it was possible to get from them, their charities had already been rewarded with titles, medals, and other distinctions,—which was the only effectual way to ensure success in the collection of money; and to obtain new honors from the authorities was very difficult.

When I returned home I went to bed, not only with a presentiment that nothing would result from my idea, but also with the shameful consciousness of having been doing something vile and contemptible the whole day. However, I did not desist.

First, the work had been begun, and false shame prevented my giving it up; second, not only the success of the enterprise itself, but even my part in it, afforded me the possibility of continuing to live in my usual way; whereas the failure of this enterprise would have put me under the constraint of giving up my present mode of life and of seeking another. Of this, I was unconsciously afraid; and therefore I refused to listen to my inner voice, and continued what I had begun.

Having sent my article to be printed, I read a proof-copy at a census-meeting in the town hall, hesitatingly, and blushing till my cheeks burned again. I felt very uncomfortable, and I saw that all my hearers were equally uncomfortable.

On my question, whether the managers of the census would accept my proposal that they should remain at their posts in order to form a link between society and those in need, an awkward silence ensued.

Then two of those present made speeches, which seemed to mend the awkwardness of my suggestions. Sympathy for me was expressed along with their general approbation, but they pointed out the impracticability of my scheme. Everyone immediately seemed more at ease; but afterwards, still wishing to succeed, I asked each district manager separately, whether during the census he was willing to investigate the needs of the poor and afterwards remain at his post in order to form this link between the poor and the rich, all were again confounded; it seemed as though their looks said, "Why, we have listened to your silly proposition out of personal regard for you; but here you come with it again!" This was the expression of their faces, but in words they told me that they consented; and two of them, separately, but as though they had agreed together, said in the same words, "We regard it as our moral duty to do so." The same impression was produced by my words upon the students who had volunteered to act as clerks during the census, when I told them that they might accomplish a charitable work besides their scientific pursuits.

When we talked the matter over I noticed that they were shy of looking me straight in the face, as one often hesitates to look into the face of a good-natured man who is talking nonsense. The same impression was produced upon the editor of the paper when I handed my article to him; also upon my son, my wife, and various other people.

Every one seemed embarrassed, but all found it necessary to approve of the idea itself; and all, immediately after this approbation, began to express their doubts as to the success of the plan, and, for some reason or other, all without exception took to condemning the indifference and coldness of society and of the world, though they evidently excluded themselves.

CHAPTER IV

By my request I was appointed to make the census of the section of Khamovnitchesky police district, near the Smolensky Market in the Prototchni Lane between the Shore Drive and Nicolsky Lane. In this district are the houses known under the name of Rzhanoff House or Rzhanoff Fortress. In bygone times these houses belonged to the merchant Rzhanoff, and are now the property of the merchants Zeemin. I had long before heard that this was considered the lowest circle of poverty and vice, which was the reason why I asked the officers of the census to assign this district to me.

My desire was gratified.

Having received the appointment from the Town Council, I went alone, a few days before the census, to inspect my district. With the help of a plan I soon found the Rzhanoff Houses,—approached by a street which terminated on the left-hand side of Nicolsky Lane—a gloomy building without any apparent entrance. From the aspect of this house I guessed it was the one I was in search of. Descending the street, I came across some boys, from ten to fourteen years old, in short coats, who were sliding down the frozen gutter, some on their feet, others upon a single skate.

The boys were ragged, and, like all town boys, sharp and bold. I stopped to look at them. An old woman in torn clothes, with hanging yellow cheeks, came round the corner. She was going up-hill to Smolensky Market, gasping painfully at every step, like a horse out of wind; and when abreast of me, stopped with hoarse, choking breath. In any other place, this old woman would have asked alms, but here she only began to talk.

"Just look at them!" she said, pointing to the sliding boys; "always at mischief! They will become the same Rzhanoff good-for-nothings as their fathers." One boy, in an overcoat and cap without a peak, overhearing her words, stopped. "You shut up!" he shouted. "You're only an old Rzhanoff goat yourself!"

I asked the boy if he lived here. "Yes, and so does she. She stole some boots," he called out, and, pushing himself off, slid on.

The old woman began a torrent of abuse, interrupted by coughs. During the squabble an old white-haired man, all in rags, came down the middle of the street, brandishing his arms, and carrying in one hand a bundle of small rusk rings. He seemed to have just fortified himself with a glass of liquor. He had evidently heard the old woman's abuse and took her side.

"I'll give it you, you little devils!" he shouted, pretending to rush after them; and, passing behind me, he stepped on the pavement. If you saw this old man in the Artat, a fashionable street, you would be struck with his air of decrepitude, feebleness, and poverty. Here he appeared as a merry workman returning from his day's labor.

I followed him. He turned round the corner to the left into Prototchni, an alley, passed the front of the house and the gate, and disappeared through the door of an inn. Into this alley opened the doors of the latter, a public-house, and several small eating-houses. It was the Rzhanoff Houses. Every thing was gray, dirty, and foul-smelling,— buildings, lodgings, courts, and people. Most of those I met here were in tattered clothes, half naked. Some were passing along, others were running from one door to another. Two were bargaining about some rags. I went round the whole building, down another lane and a court, and, having returned, stopped at the archway of the Rzhanoff Houses.

I wanted to go in and see what was going on inside, but the idea made me feel painfully awkward. If they asked me what I had come for, what should I say?

However after a little hesitation I went in. The moment I entered the court I was conscious of a most revolting stench. The court was dreadfully dirty. I turned round the corner, and at the same instant heard steps running along the boards of the gallery and down the stairs.

First a gaunt-looking woman, with tucked-up sleeves, a faded pink dress, and shoes on her stockingless feet, rushed out; after her, a rough-haired man in a red shirt, and extremely wide trousers, like a petticoat, and goloshes on his feet. The man caught her under the stairs: "You sha'n't escape me," he said, laughing.

"Just listen to the squint-eyed devil!" began the woman, who was evidently not averse to his attentions; but, having caught sight of me, she exclaimed angrily, "Who are you looking for?" As I did not want anyone in particular, I felt somewhat confused, and went away.

This little incident, though by no means remarkable in itself, suddenly showed me the work I was about to undertake in an entirely new light, especially after what I had seen on the other side of the courtyard,—the scolding woman, the light-hearted old man, and the sliding boys. I had meditated doing good to these people by the help of the rich men of Moscow. I now realized, for the first time, that all these poor unfortunates, whom I had been wishing to help, had, besides the time they spent suffering from cold and hunger in waiting to get a lodging, several hours daily to get through, and that they must somehow fill up the rest of the twenty-four hours of every day,—a whole life, of which I had never thought before. I realized now, for the first time, that all these people, besides the mere effort to find food and shelter from the cold, must live through the rest of every day of their life as other people have to do, must get angry at times, and be dull, and try to appear light-hearted, and be sad or merry. Now, for the first time (however strange the confession may sound), I was fully aware that the task which I was undertaking could not simply consist in feeding and clothing a thousand people (just as one might feed a thousand head of sheep, and drive them into shelter), but must develop some more essential help. When I considered that each one of these individuals was just another man like myself, possessing also a past history, with the same passions, temptations, and errors, the same thoughts, the same questions to be answered, then suddenly the work before me appeared stupendous and I felt my own utter helplessness;—but it had begun and I was resolved to go on.

CHAPTER V

On the appointed day, the students who were to assist me started early in the morning; while I, the philanthropist, only joined them at twelve o'clock. I could not come earlier, as I did not get up till ten, after which I had to take some coffee, and then smoke for the sake of my digestion. Twelve o'clock, then, found me at the door of the Rzhanoff Houses. A policeman showed me a public-house to which the census-clerks referred all those who wished to enquire for them. I entered, and found it very dirty and unsavoury. Here, right in front of me, was a counter; to the left a small room, furnished with tables covered with soiled napkins; to the right a large room on pillars, containing similar little tables placed in the windows and along the walls; with men here and there having tea, some very ragged, others well dressed, apparently workmen or small shopkeepers. There were also several women. In spite of the dirt, it was easy to see, by the business air of the man in charge, and the ready, obliging manners of the waiters, that the eating-house was driving a good trade. I had no sooner entered than one of the waiters was already preparing to assist me in getting off my overcoat, anxious to take my orders, and showing that evidently the people here were in the habit of doing their work quickly and readily.

My enquiry for the census-clerks was answered by a call for "Ványa" from a little man dressed in foreign fashion, who was arranging something in a cupboard behind the counter. This was the proprietor of the public-house, a peasant from Kaluga, Iván Fedotitch by name, who also rented half of the other houses, sub-letting the rooms to lodgers. In answer to his call, a thin, sallow-faced, hook-nosed lad, about eighteen years old, came forward hastily. The landlord said, "Take this gentleman to the clerks: they have gone to the main body of the building over the well."

The lad put down his napkin, pulled on a coat over his white shirt and trousers, picked up a large cap with a peak, and then, with quick, short steps, led the way by a back-door through the buildings. At the entrance of a greasy, malodorous kitchen, we met an old woman who was carefully carrying some putrid tripe in a rag. We descended into a court, built up all round with wooden buildings on stone foundations. The smell was most offensive, and seemed to be concentrated in a privy to which numbers of people were constantly resorting. This privy was really only the place which custom accepted as a privy. One could not avoid noticing this place as one passed through the courtyard. One suffered in entering the acrid atmosphere of the bad smells issuing from it.

The boy, taking care not to soil his white trousers, led me cautiously across frozen and unfrozen filth, and approached one of the buildings. The people crossing the yard and galleries all stopped to gaze at me. It was evident that a cleanly-dressed man was an unusual sight in the place.

The boy asked a woman whom we met, whether she had seen where the census officials had entered, and three people at once answered his question: some said that they were over the well; others said that they had been there, but had now gone to Nikita Ivanovitch's.

An old man in the middle of the court, who had only a shirt on, said that they were at No. 30. The boy concluded that this information was the most probable and led me to No. 30, into the basement, where darkness prevailed and a bad smell, different from that which filled the court.

We continued to descend along a dark passage. As we were traversing it a door was suddenly opened, out of which came a drunken old man in a shirt, evidently not of the peasant class. A shrieking washerwoman with tucked-up sleeves and soapy arms was pushing him out of the room. "Ványa" (my guide) shoved him aside, saying, "It won't do to kick up such a row here—and you an officer too!"

When we arrived at No. 30, Ványa pulled the door, which opened with the sound of a wet slap; and we felt a gush of soapy steam and an odor of bad food and tobacco, and entered in complete darkness. The windows were on the other side; and we were in a crooked corridor, that went right and left, with doors leading at different angles into rooms separated from it by a partition of unevenly laid boards, roughly whitewashed.

In a dark room to the left we could see a woman washing at a trough. Another old woman was looking out of a door at the right. Near an open door was a hairy, red-skinned peasant in bark shoes, sitting on a couch. His hands rested upon his knees; and he was swinging his feet and looking sadly at his shoes.

At the end of the passage a small door led into the room where the census officers had assembled. This was the room of the landlady of the whole of No. 30, who rented it from Iván Fedotitch and sub-let to ordinary or night lodgers.

In this tiny room a student sat under an image glittering with gilt paper, and, with the air of a magistrate, was putting questions to a man dressed in shirt and vest. This last was a friend of the landlady's, who was answering the questions in her stead. The landlady herself,—an old woman,—and two inquisitive lodgers, were also present.

When I entered, the room was quite filled up. I pushed through to the table, shook hands with the student, and he went on extracting his information, while I studied the inhabitants, and put questions to them for my own ends.

It appeared, however, I could find no one here upon whom to bestow my benevolence. The landlady of the rooms, notwithstanding their wretchedness and filth (which especially struck me in comparison with the mansion in which I lived), was well off, even from the point of view of town poverty; and compared with country destitution, with which I was well acquainted, she lived luxuriously. She had a feather-bed, a quilted blanket, a samovár, a fur cloak, a cupboard, with dishes, plates, etc. The landlady's friend had the same well-to-do appearance, and boasted even a watch and chain. The lodgers were poor, but among them there was no one requiring immediate help.

Three only applied for aid,—the woman washing linen, who said she had been abandoned by her husband; an old widowed woman, without means of livelihood; and the peasant in the bark shoes, who told me he had not had anything to eat that day. But, upon gathering more precise information, it became evident that all these people were not in extreme want, and that, before one could really help, it would be necessary to make their more intimate acquaintance.

When I offered the washerwoman to place her children in a "home," she became confused, thought over it some time, then thanked me much, but evidently did not desire it; she would rather have had some money. Her eldest daughter helped her in the washing, and the second acted as nurse to the little boy.

The old woman asked to be put into a refuge; but, examining her corner, I saw she was not in extreme distress. She had a box containing some property and a teapot, two cups, and old bon-bon boxes with tea and sugar. She knitted stockings and gloves, and received a monthly allowance from a lady benefactress.

The peasant was evidently more desirous of wetting his throat after his last day's drunkenness than of food, and anything given him would have gone to the public-house. In these rooms, therefore, there was no one whom I could have rendered in any respect happier by helping them with money.

There were only paupers there,—and paupers, it seemed, of a questionable kind.

I put down the names of the old woman, the laundress, and the peasant, and settled in my mind that it would be necessary to do something for them, but that first I would help those other *especially* unfortunate ones whom I expected to come across in this house. I made up my mind that some system was necessary in distributing the aid which we had to give: first, we must find the most needy, and then come to such as these.

But in the next lodging, and in the next again, I found only similar cases, which would have to be looked into more closely before being helped. Of those whom pecuniary aid alone would have rendered happy, I found none.

However ashamed I feel in confessing it, I began to experience a certain disappointment at not finding in these houses anything resembling what I had expected. I thought to find very exceptional people; but, when I had gone over all the lodgings, I became convinced that their inhabitants were in no way extremely peculiar, but much like those amongst whom I lived.

As with us, so also with them, there were some more or less good and others more or less bad: there were some more or less happy and others more or less unhappy. Those who were unhappy amongst them would have been equally wretched with us, their misery being within themselves,—a misery not to be mended by any kind of bank-note.

CHAPTER VI

The inhabitants of these houses belonged to the lowest population of the town, which in Moscow amounts to perhaps more than a hundred thousand. In this house, there were representative men of all kinds,—petty employers and journeymen, shoemakers, brushmakers, joiners, hackney coachmen, jobbers carrying on business on their own account, washerwomen, second-hand dealers, money-lenders, day-laborers, and others without any definite occupation; and here also lodged beggars and unfortunate women.

Many who were like the people I had seen waiting at Liapin's house lived here, mixed up with the working-people. But those whom I saw then were in a most wretched condition, having eaten and drunk all they had, and, turned out of the public-house, were waiting, as for heavenly manna, cold and hungry, to be admitted into the free night-lodging-house,—and longing day by day to be taken to prison, in order to be sent back to their homes. Here I saw the same men among a greater number of working-people, at a time when by some means or other they had got a few farthings to pay for their night's lodging, and perhaps a ruble or two for food and drink.

However strange it may sound, I had no such feelings here as I experienced in Liapin's house; on the contrary, during my first visiting-round, I and the students had a sensation which was rather agreeable than otherwise. Why do I say "almost agreeable?" It is not true. The sensation called forth by the companionship of these men—strange as it may seem—was simply a very agreeable one.

The first impression was, that the majority of the lodgers here were working people, and very kindly disposed. We found most of them at work,—the washerwomen at their tubs, the joiners by their benches, the bootmakers at their lasts. The tiny rooms were full of people, and the work was going on cheerfully and with energy. There was a smell of perspiration among the workmen, of leather at the bootmaker's, of chips in the carpenter's shop. We often heard songs, and saw bare, sinewy arms working briskly and skilfully.

Everywhere we were received kindly and cheerfully. Nearly everywhere our intrusion into the daily life of these people excited no desire in them to show us their importance, or to rate us soundly, which happens when such visits are paid to the lodgings of well-to-do people. On the contrary, all our questions were answered simply, without any particular importance being attached to them,—served, indeed, only as an excuse for merriment and for jokes about how they were to be enrolled on the list, how such a one was as good as two, and how two others ought to be reckoned as one.

Many we found at dinner or at tea; and each time, in answer to our greeting, "Bread and salt," or, "Tea and sugar," they said, "You are welcome"; and some even made room for us to sit down. Instead of the place being the resort of an ever-shifting population, such as we expected to find, it turned out that in this house were many rooms which had been tenanted by the same people for long periods.

One carpenter, with his workmen, and a bootmaker, with his journeymen, had been living here for ten years. The bootmaker's shop was very dirty and quite choked up, but all his men were working very cheerily. I tried to talk with one of the workmen, wishing to sound him about the miseries of his lot, what he owed to the master, and so forth; but he did not understand me, and spoke of his master and of his life from a very favourable point of view.

In one lodging, there lived an old man with his old wife. They dealt in apples. Their room was warm, clean, and filled with their belongings. The floor was covered with straw-matting which they got from the apple stores. There were chests, a cupboard, a samovár, and crockery. In the corner were many holy images, before which two lamps were burning: on the wall hung fur cloaks wrapped up in a sheet. The old woman with wrinkled face, kind and talkative, was apparently quite delighted with her quiet, respectable life.

Iván Fedotitch, the owner of the inn and of the lodgings, came out and walked with us. He joked kindly with many of the lodgers, calling them all by their names, and giving us short sketches of their characters. They were as other men, did not consider themselves unhappy, but believed they were like everyone else, as in reality they were. We were prepared to see only dreadful things, and we met instead objects not only not repulsive, but estimable. There were so many of these, compared with the ragged, ruined, unoccupied people we met now and then among them, that the latter did not in the least destroy the general impression. To the students it did not appear so remarkable as it did to me. They were merely performing an act useful to science, as they thought; and, in passing, made casual observations: but I was a benefactor; my object in going there was to help the unhappy, ruined, depraved men and women whom I had expected to meet in this house. Suddenly, instead of unhappy, ruined, depraved beings, I found the majority to be workingmen: quiet, satisfied, cheerful, kind, and very good.

I was still more strongly impressed when I found that in these lodgings the crying want I wished to relieve had already been relieved before I came. But by whom? By these same unhappy, depraved beings whom I was prepared to save! And this help was given in a way not open to me.

In one cellar lay a lonely old man suffering from typhus-fever. He had no connections in the world; yet a woman,—a widow with a little girl,—quite a stranger to him, but living in the corner next to him, nursed him, gave him tea, and bought him medicine with her own money.

In another lodging lay a woman in puerperal fever. A woman of the town was nursing her child, and had prepared a sucking-bottle for him, and had not gone out to ply her sad trade for two days.

An orphan girl was taken into the family of a tailor, who had three children of his own. Thus, there remained only such miserable unoccupied men as retired officials, clerks, men-servants out of situations, beggars, tipsy people, prostitutes, children, whom it was not possible to help all at once by means of money, but whose cases it was necessary to consider carefully before assisting them. I had been seeking for men suffering immediately from want of means, whom one might be able to help by sharing one's superfluities with them. I had not found them. All whom I had seen, it would have been very difficult to assist materially without devoting time and care to their cases.

CHAPTER VII

These unfortunate necessitous ones ranged themselves in my mind under three heads: First, those who had lost former advantageous positions, and who were waiting to return to them (such men belonged to the lowest as well as to the highest classes of society); Secondly, women of the town, who are very numerous in these houses; and Thirdly, children.

The majority of those I found, and noted down, were men who had lost former places, and were desirous of returning to them, chiefly of the better class, and government officials. In almost all the lodgings we entered with the landlord, we were told, "Here we need not trouble to fill up the card ourselves: the man here is able to do it, provided he is not tipsy."

Thus summoned by Iván Fedotitch, there would appear, from some dark corner, the once rich nobleman or official, mostly drunk, and always half-dressed. If he were not drunk, he willingly undertook the task: he kept nodding his head with a sense of importance, knitted his brows, inserted now and then learned terms in his remarks, and carefully holding in his dirty, trembling hands the neat pink card, looked round at his fellow-lodgers with pride and contempt, as if he were now, by the superiority of his education, triumphing over those who had been continually humbling him.

He was evidently pleased to have intercourse with the world which used pink cards, with a world of which he himself had once been a member.

To my questions about his life, this kind of man not only replied willingly, but with enthusiasm,—beginning to tell a story, fixed in his mind like a prayer, about all kinds of misfortunes which had happened to him, and chiefly about his former position, in which, considering his education, he ought to have remained.

Many such people are scattered about in all the tenements of the Rzhanoff Houses. One lodging-house was tenanted exclusively by them, women and men. As we approached them, Iván Fedotitch said, "Now, here's where the nobility live."

The lodging was full. Almost all the lodgers—about forty persons—were at home. In the whole house, there were no faces so ruined and degraded-looking as these,—if old, flabby; if young, pale and haggard.

I talked with several of them. Almost always the same story was told, differing only in degree of development. One and all had been once rich, or had still a rich father or brother or uncle; or either his father or his unfortunate self had held a high office. Then came some misfortune caused by envious enemies, or his own imprudent kindness, or some out-of-the-way occurrence; and, having lost everything, he was obliged to descend to these strange and hateful surroundings, among lice and rags, in company with drunkards and loose characters, feeding upon bread and liver, and subsisting by beggary.

All the thoughts, desires, and recollections of these men are turned toward the past. The present appears to them as something unnatural, hideous, and unworthy of attention. It does not exist for them. They have only recollections of the past, and expectations of the future which may be realized at any moment, and for the attainment of which but very little is needed; but, unfortunately, this little is out of their reach; it cannot be got anywhere: and so one has wasted one year, another five, and a third thirty years.

One needs only to be dressed respectably in order to call on a well-known person who is kindly disposed toward him; another requires only to be dressed, have his debts paid, and go to some town or other; a third wants to take his effects out of pawn, and get a small sum to carry on a law-suit, which must be decided in his favour, and then all will be well again. All say that they have need of some external circumstance in order to regain that position which they think natural and happy.

If I had not been blinded by my pride in being a benefactor, I should have needed only to look a little closer into their faces, young and old, which were generally weak, sensual, but kind, in order to understand that their misfortunes could not be met by external means; that they could be happy in no position while their present conception of life remained the same; that they were by no means peculiar people in peculiarly unhappy circumstances, but that they were like all other men, ourselves included.

I remember well how my intercourse with men of this class was particularly trying to me. I now understand why it was so. In them I saw my own self as in a mirror. If I had considered carefully my own life and the lives of people of my own class, I should have seen that between us and these unfortunate men there existed no essential difference.

Those who live around me in expensive suites of apartments and houses of their own in the best streets of the city, eating something better than liver or herring with their bread, are none the less unhappy. They also are discontented with their lot, regret the past, and desire a happier future, precisely as did the wretched tenants of the Rzhanoff Houses. Both wished to be worked less and to be worked for more, the difference between them being only in degrees of idleness.

Unfortunately, I did not see this at first, nor did I understand that such people needed to be relieved, not by my charity, but from their own false views of the world; and that to change a man's estimate of life he must be given one more accurate than his own, which, unhappily, not possessing myself, I could not communicate to others.

These men were unhappy not because, to use an illustration, they were without nourishing food, but because their stomachs were spoiled; and they required, not nourishment, but a tonic. I did not see that in order to help them, it was not necessary to give them food but to teach them how to eat. Though I am anticipating, I must say that of all these people whose names I put down I did not in reality help one, notwithstanding that everything some of them had desired was done to relieve them. Of these I became acquainted with three men in particular. All three, after many failures and much assistance, are now in the same position they were in three years ago.

CHAPTER VIII

The second class of unfortunates, whom I hoped afterwards to be able to help, were women of the town. These women were very numerous in the Rzhanoff Houses; and they were of every kind, from young girls still bearing some likeness to women, to old and fearful-looking creatures without a vestige of humanity. The hope of helping these women, whom I had not at first in view, was aroused by the following circumstances.

When we had finished half of our tour, we had already acquired a somewhat mechanical method. On entering a new lodging we at once asked for the landlord. One of us sat down, clearing a space to write; and the other went from one to another, questioning each man and woman in the room, and reporting the information obtained to him who was writing.

On our entering one of the basement lodgings, the student went to look for the landlord; and I began to question all who were in the place. This place was divided thus: In the middle of the room, which was four yards square, there stood a stove. From the stove four partitions or screens radiated, making a similar number of small compartments. In the first of these, which had two doors in it opposite each other, and four pallets, were an old man and a woman. Next to this was a rather long but narrow room, in which was the landlord, a young, pale, good-looking man dressed in a gray woollen coat. To the left of the first division was a third small room where a man was sleeping, seemingly tipsy, and a woman in a pink dressing-gown. The fourth compartment was behind a partition, access to it being through the landlord's room.

The student entered the latter, while I remained in the first, questioning the old man and the woman. The former had been a compositor, but now had no means of livelihood whatever.

The woman was a cook's wife.

I went into the third compartment, and asked the woman in the dressing-gown about the man who was asleep.

She answered that he was a visitor.

I asked her who she was.

She replied that she was a peasant girl from the county of Moscow.

"What is your occupation?" She laughed, and made no answer.

"What do you do for your living?" I repeated, thinking she had not understood the question.

"I sit in the inn," she said.

I did not understand her, and asked again,—

"What are your means of living?"

She gave me no answer, but continued to giggle. In the fourth room, where we had not yet been, I heard the voices of women also giggling.

The landlord came out of his room, and approached us. He had evidently heard my questions and the woman's answers. He glanced sternly at her, and, turning to me, said, "She is a prostitute"; and it was evident that he was pleased that he knew this word,—which is the one used in official circles,—and at having pronounced it correctly. And having said this with a respectful smile of satisfaction towards me, he turned to the woman. As he did so, the expression of his face changed. In a peculiarly contemptuous manner, and with rapid utterance as one would speak to a dog, he said, without looking at her, "Don't be a fool! instead of saying you sit in the inn, speak plainly, and say you are a prostitute.—She does not even yet know her proper name," he said, turning to me.

This manner of speaking shocked me.

"It is not for us to shame her," I said. "If we were all living according to God's commandment, there would be no such persons."

"There are such doings," said the landlord, with an artificial smile.

"Therefore we must pity them, and not reproach them. Is it their fault?"

I do not remember exactly what I said. I remember only that I was disgusted by the disdainful tone of this young landlord, in a lodging filled with females whom he termed prostitutes; and I pitied the woman, and expressed both feelings.

No sooner had I said this, than I heard from the small compartment where the giggling had been, the noise of creaking bed-boards; and over the partition, which did not reach to the ceiling, appeared the dishevelled curly head of a female with small swollen eyes, and a shining red face; a second, and then a third, head followed. They were evidently standing on their beds; and all three were stretching their necks and holding their breath, and looking silently at me with strained attention.

A painful silence followed.

The student, who had been smiling before this happened, now became grave; the landlord became confused, and cast down his eyes; and the women continued to look at me in expectation.

I felt more disconcerted than all the rest. I had certainly not expected that a casual word would produce such an effect. It was like the field of battle covered with dead bones seen by the prophet Ezekiel, on which, trembling from contact with the spirit, the dead bones began to move. I had casually uttered a word of love and pity, which produced upon all such an effect that it seemed as if they had been only waiting for it, to cease to be corpses, and to become alive again.

They continued to look at me, as if wondering what would come next, as if waiting for me to say those words and do those acts by which these dry bones would begin to come together,—be covered with flesh and receive life.

But I felt, alas! that I had no such words or deeds to give, or to continue as I had begun. In the depth of my soul I felt that I had told a lie, that I myself was like them, that I had nothing more to say; and I began to write down on the card the names and the occupations of all the lodgers there.

This occurrence led me into a new kind of error. I began to think that these unhappy creatures also could be helped. This, in my self deception, it seemed to me would be very easily done. I said to myself, "Now we shall put down the names of these women too; and afterwards, when we (though it never occurred to me to ask who were the *we*) have written everything down, we can occupy ourselves with their affairs." I imagined that *we*, the very persons who, during many generations, have been leading such women into such a condition, and still continue to do so, could one fine morning wake up and remedy it all. And yet, if I could have recollected my conversation with the lost woman who was nursing the baby for the sick mother, I should have understood the folly of such an idea.

When we first saw this woman nursing the child, we thought that it was hers; but upon our asking her what she was, she answered us plainly that she was a wench. She did not say "prostitute." It was left for the proprietor of the lodgings to make use of that terrible word.

The supposition that she had a child gave me the idea of helping her out of her present position.

"Is this child yours?" I asked.

"No: it is that woman's there."

"Why do you nurse him?"

"She asked me to. She is dying."

Though my surmise turned out to be wrong, I continued to speak with her in the same spirit. I began to question her as to who she was, and how she came to be in such a position. She told me her story willingly, and very plainly. She belonged to the artisan class of Moscow, the daughter of a factory workman. She was left an orphan, and adopted by her aunt, from whose house she began to visit the inns. The aunt was now dead.

When I asked her whether she wished to change her course of life, my question did not even interest her. How can a supposition about something quite impossible awaken an interest in any one? She smiled and said,—

"Who would take me with a yellow ticket?"

"But," said I, "if it were possible to find you a situation as a cook or something else?" I said this because she looked like a strong woman, with a kind, dull, round face, not unlike many cooks I had seen.

Evidently my words did not please her. She repeated, "Cook! but I do not understand how to bake bread."

She spoke jestingly; but, by the expression of her face, I saw that she was unwilling; that she even considered the position and rank of a cook beneath her.

This woman, who, in the most simple manner, like the widow in the gospel, had sacrificed all that she had for a sick person, at the same time, like other women of the same profession, considered the position of a workman or workwoman low and despicable. She had been educated to live without work,—a life which all her friends considered quite natural. This was her misfortune. And by this she came into her present position, and is kept in it. This brought her to the inns. Who of us men and women will cure her of this false view of life? Are there among us any men convinced that a laborious life is more respectable than an idle one, and who are living according to this conviction, and who make this the test of their esteem and respect?

If I had thought about it I should have understood that neither I nor anybody else I know, was able to cure a person of this disease.

I should have understood that those wondering and awakened faces that looked over the partition expressed merely astonishment at the pity shown to them, but no wish to reform their lives. They did not see the immorality. They knew that they were despised and condemned, but the reason for this they could not understand. They had lived in this manner from their infancy among women like themselves, who, they know very well, have always existed, do exist, and are necessary to society, that there are officials deputed by government to see that they conform to regulations.

Besides, they know that they have power over men, and subdue them, and often influence them more than any other women. They see that their position in society, notwithstanding the fact that they are always blamed, is recognised by men as well as by women and by the government; and therefore they cannot even understand of what they have to repent, and wherein they should reform.

During one of our tours the student told me that in one of the lodgings there was a woman who sends out her daughter, thirteen years old, to walk the streets. Wishing to save this little girl I went on purpose to their lodging.

Mother and daughter were living in great poverty. The mother, a small, dark-complexioned prostitute of forty years of age, was not simply ugly, but disagreeably ugly. The daughter was also bad-looking. To all my indirect questions about their mode of life, the mother replied curtly, with a look of suspicion and animosity, apparently feeling that I was an enemy with bad intentions: the daughter said nothing without looking first at the mother, in whom she evidently had entire confidence.

They did not awaken pity in my heart, but rather disgust. Still I decided that it was necessary to save the daughter, to awaken an interest in ladies who might sympathize with the miserable condition of these women and might so be brought here.

Yet if I had thought about the antecedents of the mother, how she had given birth to her daughter, how she had fed and brought her up, certainly without any outside help, and with great sacrifices to herself; if I had thought of the view of life which had formed itself in her mind,—I should have understood, that, in the mother's conduct, there was nothing at all bad or immoral, seeing she had been doing for her daughter all she could; i.e., what she considered best for herself.

It was possible to take this girl away from her mother by force; but to convince her that she was doing wrong in selling her daughter was not possible. It would first be necessary to save this woman—this mother—from a condition of life approved by every one, and according to which a woman may live without marrying and without working, serving exclusively as a gratification to the passions. If I had thought about this, I should have understood that the majority of those ladies whom I wished to send here for saving this girl were not only themselves avoiding family duties, and leading idle and sensuous lives, but were consciously educating their daughters for this very same mode of existence. One mother leads her daughter to the inn, and another to court and to balls. Both the views of the world held by both mothers are the same; viz., that a woman must gratify the passions of men, and for that she must be fed, dressed, and taken care of.

How, then, are our ladies to reform this woman and her daughter?

CHAPTER IX

Still more strange were my dealings with the children. In my *rôle* as benefactor I paid attention to the children too, wishing to save innocent beings from going to ruin in this den; and I wrote down their names in order to attend to them myself *afterwards*.

Among these children my attention was particularly drawn to Serozha, a boy twelve years old. I sincerely pitied this clever, intelligent lad, who had been living with a bootmaker, and who was left without any place of refuge when his master was put into prison. I wished to do something for him.

I will now give the result of my benevolence in his case, because this boy's story will show my false position as a benefactor better than anything else.

I took the boy into my house, and lodged him in the kitchen. Could I possibly bring a lousy boy out of a den of depravity to my children? I considered that I had been very kind in having put him where he was, amongst my servants. I thought myself a great benefactor for having given him some of my old clothes and fed him; though it was properly my cook who did it, not I. The boy remained in my house about a week.

During this week I saw him twice, and, passing him, spoke some words to him, and, when out walking, called on a bootmaker whom I knew and proposed the boy as an apprentice. A peasant who was on a visit at my house invited him to go to his village and work in a family. The boy refused to accept it and disappeared within a week.

I went to Rzhanoff's house to enquire after him. He had returned there; but when I called, he was not at home. He had already been two days in a menagerie in Presnem Ponds, where he hired himself for 6d. a day to appear in a procession of savages in costume, leading an elephant. There was some public show on at the time.

I went to see him again, but he was so ungrateful, he evidently avoided me. Had I reflected upon the life of this boy and on my own, I should have understood that the boy had been spoiled by the fact of his having tasted the sweets of a merry and idle life, and that he had lost the habit of working. And I, in order to confer on him a benefit and reform him, took him into my own house. And what did he see there? He saw my children, some older than he, some younger, and some of the same age, who not only never did anything for themselves, but gave as much work to others as they could. They dirtied and spoiled everything about them, surfeited themselves with all sorts of dainties, broke the china, upset and threw to the dogs food which would have been a treat to him. If I took him out of a den and brought him to a respectable place, he could not but assimilate the views of life which existed there; and, according to these views, he understood that in a respectable position one must live without working, eat and drink well, and lead a merry life.

True, he did not know that my children had much labour in learning the exceptions in Latin and Greek grammars; nor would he have been able to understand the object of such work. But one cannot help seeing that even had he understood it the influence upon him of the example of my children would have been still stronger. He would have then understood that they were being educated in such a way, that, not working now, they might afterwards also work as little as possible, and enjoy the good things of life by virtue of their diplomas.

But what he did understand of it made him go, not to the peasant to take care of cattle and feed on potatoes and kvas, but to the menagerie in the costume of a savage to lead an elephant for 6d. a day. I ought to have understood how foolish it was of one who was educating his own children in complete idleness and luxury to try to reform other men and their children, and save them from going to ruin and idleness in what I called the *dens* in Rzhanoff's house; where, however, three-fourths of the men were working for themselves and for others. But then I understood nothing of all this.

In Rzhanoff's house there were a great many children in the most miserable condition. There were children of prostitutes, orphans, and children carried about the streets by beggars. They were all very wretched. But my experience with Serozha showed me that so long as I continued living the life I did I was not able to help them.

While the boy was living with us I remember I took pains to hide from him our way of life, particularly that of my children. I felt that all my endeavours to lead him to a good and laborious life were frustrated by my example and that of my children. It is very easy to take away a child from a prostitute or a beggar. It is very easy, when one has money, to wash him, dress him in new clothes, feed him well, and even teach him different accomplishments; but to teach him how to earn his living, is, for us who have not been earning ours but doing just the contrary, not only difficult but quite impossible, because by our example and by the very improvements of his mode of life effected by us without any cost on our part, we teach him the very opposite.

You may take a puppy, pet him, feed him, teach him to carry things after you, and be pleased with looking at him: but it is not enough to feed a man, dress him, and teach him Greek; you must teach him how to live; i.e., how to take less from others and give them more in return: and yet through our own mode of life we cannot help teaching him the very opposite whether we take him into our house or put him into a home to bring up.

CHAPTER X

I have never since experienced such a feeling of compassion towards men and of aversion towards myself, as I felt in Liapin's house. I was now filled with the desire to carry out the scheme I had already begun and to do good to the men whom I had met.

And, strange to say, though it might seem that to do good and to give money to those in want of it was a good deed, and ought to dispose men to universal love, it turned out quite the reverse; calling up in me bitter feelings and disposition to censure them. Even during our first tour a scene occurred similar to that in Liapin's house; but it failed to produce again the same effect and created a very different impression.

It began with my finding in one of the lodgings a miserable person who required immediate help,—a woman who had not eaten food for two days.

It happened thus: In one very large and almost empty night-lodging, I asked an old woman whether there were any poor people who had nothing to eat. She hesitated a moment and then named two; then suddenly, as if recollecting herself, she said, "Yes, there lies one of them," pointing to a pallet. "This one," she added, "indeed, has nothing to eat."

"You don't say so! Who is she?"

"She has been a lost woman; but as nobody takes her now, she can't earn anything. The landlady has had pity on her, but now she wants to turn her out.—Agafia! I say, Agafia!" cried the old woman.

We went a little nearer, and saw something rise from the pallet. This was a grey-haired, dishevelled woman, thin as a skeleton, in a dirty, torn chemise, and with peculiarly glittering, immovable eyes. She looked fixedly beyond us, tried to snatch up her jacket behind her in order to cover her bony chest, and growled out like a dog, "What? what?"

I asked her how she managed to live. For some time she was unable to see the drift of my words and said, "I don't know myself; they are going to turn me out."

I asked again; and oh, how ashamed of myself I feel! my hand can scarcely write it! I asked her whether it was true that she was starving. She replied in the same feverish, excited manner, "I had nothing to eat yesterday; I have had nothing to eat to-day."

The miserable aspect of this woman impressed me deeply, but quite differently from those in Liapin's house: there, out of pity for them, I felt embarrassed and ashamed of myself; but here, I rejoiced that I had at last found what I had been looking for,—a hungry being.

I gave her a ruble and I remember how glad I felt that the others had seen it.

The old woman forthwith asked me also for money. It was so pleasant to me to give that I handed her some also, without thinking whether it was necessary or not. She accompanied me to the door, and those who were in the corridor heard how she thanked me. Probably my questions about the poor provoked expectations, for some of the inmates began to follow us wherever we went.

Among those that begged, there were evidently drunkards, who gave me a most disagreeable impression; but having once given to the old woman I thought I had no right to refuse them, and I began to give away more. This only increased the number of applicants, and there was a stir throughout the whole lodging-house.

On the stairs and in the galleries, people appeared dogging my steps. When I came out of the yard, a boy ran quickly down the stairs, pushing through the people. He did not notice me and said hurriedly,—

"He gave a ruble to Agafia!"

Having reached the ground, he, too, joined the crowd that was following me. I came out into the street. All sorts of people crowded round begging for money. Having given away all I had in coppers, I entered a shop and asked the proprietor to give me change for ten rubles.

Here occurred a scene similar to that which took place in Liapin's house. A dreadful confusion ensued. Old women, seedy gentlefolk, peasants, children, all crowded about the shop, stretching out their hands; I gave, and asked some of them about their position and means, and entered all in my note-book. The shopkeeper, having turned up the fur collar of his great-coat, was sitting like a statue, glancing now and then at the crowd, and again staring beyond it. He apparently felt like everyone else, that all this was very foolish, but he dared not say so.

In Liapin's house the misery and humiliation of the people had overwhelmed me; and I felt myself to blame for it, and also the desire and the possibility of becoming a better man. But though the scene here was similar, it produced quite a different effect. In the first place, I felt angry with many of those who assailed me, and then anxious as to what the shopmen and the dvorniks might think of me. I returned home that day with a weight on my mind. I knew that what I had done was foolish and inconsistent; but, as usual when my conscience was troubled, I talked the more about my projected plan, as if I had no doubt whatever as to its success.

The next day I went alone to those whom I had noted down, and who seemed the most miserable, thinking they could be more easily helped than others.

As I have already mentioned, I was not really able to help any of these people. It turned out that to do so was more difficult than I had imagined: in short, I only tormented these men and helped no one.

Before the last visiting-tour I went several times to Rzhanoff's house, and each time the same thing occurred: I was assailed by a crowd of men and women in the midst of whom I utterly lost my presence of mind.

I felt the impossibility of doing anything because there were so many of them; besides, each of them, taken separately, did not awaken any sympathy in me. I felt that every one lied, or at least prevaricated, and regarded me only as a purse out of which money could be drawn. It often seemed to me that the very money extorted from me did not improve their position but only made it worse.

The oftener I went to these houses, the closer the intercourse which I had with the inmates, the more apparent became the impossibility of doing anything; but notwithstanding this, I did not give up my plan until after the last night tour with the census-takers.

I feel more ashamed of this visit than of any other. Formerly I had gone alone, but now twenty of us went together. At seven o'clock all who wished to take part in this last tour began to assemble in my house. They were almost all strangers to me. Some students, an officer, and two of my fashionable acquaintances, who, after having repeated the usual phrase, "C'est très intéressant!" asked me to put them into the number of the census-takers.

These fashionable friends of mine had dressed themselves in shooting-jackets and tall travelling boots, which they thought more suited to the visit than their ordinary clothes. They carried with them peculiar pocket-books and extraordinary-looking pencils. They were in that agitated state of mind which one experiences just before going to a hunt, or to a duel, or into a battle. The falseness and foolishness of our enterprise was now more apparent to me in looking at them; but were we not all in the same ridiculous position?

Before starting we had a conference, somewhat like a council of war, as to what we should begin with, how to divide ourselves, and so on. This conference was just like all other official councils, meetings, and committees: each spoke, not because he had anything to say, or to ask, but because every one tried to find something to say in order not to be behind the rest. But during the conversation no one alluded to the acts of benevolence to which I had so many times referred; and however much ashamed I felt, I found it was needful to remind them that we must carry out our charitable intentions by writing down, during the visiting-tour, the names of all whom we should find in a destitute condition.

I had always felt ashamed to speak about these matters; but here, in the midst of our hurried preparations for the expedition, I could scarcely utter a word about them. All listened to me and seemed touched, all agreed with me in words; but it was evident that each of them knew that it was folly, and that it would lead to nothing, and so they began at once to talk about other subjects, and continued doing so until it was time for us to start.

We came to the dark tavern, aroused the waiters, and began to sort out papers. When we were told that the people, having heard about this visiting-tour, had begun to leave their lodgings, we asked the landlord to shut the gate, and we ourselves went to the yard to persuade those to remain who wanted to escape, assuring them that no one would ask to see their passports.

I remember the strange and painful impression produced upon me by these frightened night-lodgers. Ragged and half-dressed, they all appeared tall by the light of the lantern in the dark court-yard. Frightened and horrible in their terror, they stood in a small knot round the pestilential out-house, listening to our persuasions, but not believing us; and, evidently, like hunted animals, prepared to do anything to escape from us.

Gentlemen of all kinds, town and country policemen, public coroner and judges, had, all their lives, been hunting them in towns and villages, on the roads and in the streets, in the taverns and in the lodging-houses, and suddenly these gentlemen had come at night and shut the gate, only, forsooth, in order to count them! They found this as difficult to believe as it would be for hares to believe that the dogs had come out not to catch but to count them.

But the gates were shut, and the frightened night-lodgers returned to their places; and we, having separated into groups, began our visit. With me were my fashionable acquaintances and two students. Ványa, with a lantern, went before us in a great-coat and white trousers, and we followed. We entered lodgings well known to me. The place was familiar, some of the persons also; but the majority were new to me, and the spectacle was also a new and dreadful one,—still more dreadful than that which I had seen at Liapin's house. All the lodgings were filled, all the pallets occupied, and not only by one, but often by two persons. The sight was dreadful, because of the closeness with which these people were huddled together, and because of the indiscriminate commingling of men and women. Such of the latter as were not dead-drunk were sleeping with men. Many women with children slept with strange men on narrow beds.

The spectacle was dreadful, owing to the misery, dirt, raggedness, and terror of these people; and chiefly because there were so many of them. One lodging, then another, then a third, a tenth, a twentieth, and so on, without end. And everywhere the same fearful stench, the same suffocating exhalation, the same confusion of sexes, men and women, drunk, or in a state of insensibility; the same terror, submissiveness, and guilt stamped on all faces, so that I felt deeply ashamed and grieved, as I had before at Liapin's. At last I understood that what I was about to do was disgusting, foolish, and therefore impossible; so I left off writing down their names and questioning them, knowing now that nothing would come of it.

I felt deeply hurt.

At Liapin's I had been like a man who sees a horrible wound on the body of another. He feels sorry for the man, ashamed of not having relieved him before, yet he can still hope to help the sufferer; but now I was like a doctor who comes with his own medicines to the patient, uncovers his wound only to mangle it, and to confess to himself that all he has done has been done in vain, and that his remedy is ineffectual.

CHAPTER XI

This visit gave the last blow to my self-deception. It became very evident to me that my aim was not only foolish, but even productive of evil. Yet, though I knew this, it seemed my duty to continue the project a little longer: first, because of the article I had written and by my visits I had raised the expectations of the poor; secondly, because what I had said and written had awakened the sympathy of some benefactors, many of whom had promised to assist me personally and with money. And I was expecting to be applied to by both, and hoped to satisfy them as well as I was able.

As regards the applications made to me by those who were in need, the following details may be given: I received more than a hundred letters, which came exclusively from the "rich poor," if I may so express myself. Some of them I visited, and some I left unanswered. In no instance did I succeed in doing any good. All the applications made to me were from persons who were once in a privileged position (I call such persons privileged who receive more from others than they give in return), had lost that position, and were desirous of regaining it. One wanted two hundred rubles in order to keep his business from going to ruin, and to enable him to finish the education of his children; another wanted to have a photographic establishment; a third wanted money to pay his debts, and take his best clothes out of pawn; a fourth was in need of a piano, in order to perfect himself and to earn money to support his family by giving lessons. The majority did not name any particular sum of money: they simply asked for help; but when I began to investigate what was necessary, it turned out that their wants increased in proportion to the help offered, and nothing satisfactorily resulted. I repeat again, the fault may have been in my want of understanding; but in any case I helped no one, notwithstanding the fact that I made every effort to do so.

As for the philanthropists who were to co-operate with me, something very strange and quite unexpected occurred: of all who promised to assist with money, and even stated the amount they would give, not one contributed anything for distribution among the poor.

The promises of pecuniary assistance amounted to about three thousand rubles; but of all these people, not one recollected his agreement, or gave me a single kopek. The students alone gave the money which they received as payment for visiting, about twelve rubles; so that my scheme, which was to have collected tens of thousands of rubles from the rich, and to have saved hundreds and thousands of people from misery and vice, ended in my distributing at random some few rubles offered by the students, with twenty-five more sent me by the town-council for my labour as manager, which I positively did not know what to do with.

So ended the affair.

Then, before leaving Moscow for the country, on the Sunday before the Carnival, I went to the Rzhanoff house in the morning in order to distribute the thirty-seven rubles among the poor. I visited all whom I knew in the lodgings, but found only one invalid, to whom I gave something,—five rubles, I think. There was nobody else to give to. Of course, many began to beg; but, as I did not know them, I made up my mind to take the advice of Iván Fedotitch, the tavern-keeper, respecting the distribution of the remaining thirty-two rubles.

It was the first day of the carnival. Everybody was smartly dressed, all had had food, and many were drunk. In the yard near the corner of the house stood an old-clothes man, dressed in a ragged peasant's coat and bark shoes. He was still hale and hearty. Sorting his purchases, he was putting them into different heaps,—leather, iron, and other things,—and was singing a merry song at the top of his voice.

I began to talk with him. He was seventy years of age; had no relatives; earned his living by dealing in old clothes, and not only did not complain, but said he had enough to eat, drink, and to spare. I asked him who in the place were particularly in want. He became cross, and said plainly that there was no one in want but drunkards and idlers; but on learning my object in asking, he begged me five kopeks for drink, and ran to the tavern for it.

I also went to the tavern to see Iván Fedotitch, to ask him to distribute the money for me. It was full; gayly-dressed tipsy prostitutes were walking to and fro; all the tables were occupied; many people were already drunk; and in the small room someone was playing a harmonium, and two people were dancing. Iván Fedotitch, out of respect for me, ordered them to leave off, and sat down next me at a vacant table. I asked him, as he knew his lodgers well, to point out those most in want, as I was intrusted with a little money for distribution, and wished him to direct me. The kind-hearted man (he died a year after) gave me his attention for a time in order to oblige me, although he had to wait on his customers. He began to think it over, and was evidently puzzled. One old waiter had overheard us, and took his part in the conference.

They began to go over his lodgers, some of whom were known to me, but they could not agree. "Paramonovna," suggested the waiter.

"Well; yes, she does go hungry sometimes; but she drinks."

"What difference does that make?"

"Well, Spiridon Ivanovitch, he has children; that's the man for you."

But Iván Fedotitch had doubts about Spiridon too.

"Akulina, but she has a pension. Ah, but there is the blind man!"

To him I myself objected: I had just seen him. This was an old man of eighty years of age, without any relatives. One could scarcely imagine any condition to be worse; and yet I had just seen him lying drunk on a feather bed, cursing at his comparatively young mistress in the most filthy language.

They then named a one-armed boy and his mother. I saw that Iván Fedotitch was in great difficulty owing to his conscientiousness, for he knew that every thing given away by me would be spent at his tavern. But as I had to get rid of my thirty-two rubles, I insisted, and we managed somehow or other to distribute the money. Those who received it were mostly well-dressed, and we had not far to go to find them: they were all in the tavern. The one-armed boy came in top-boots and a red shirt and waistcoat.

Thus ended all my benevolent enterprises; and I left for the country vexed with everyone, as it always happens when one does something foolish and harmful. Nothing came of it all, except the train of thoughts and feelings which it called forth in me, which not only did not cease, but doubly agitated my mind.

CHAPTER XII

What did it all mean?

I had lived in the country and had entered into relations with the country-poor. It is not out of false modesty, but that I may state the truth, which is necessary in order to understand the run of all my thoughts and feelings, that I must say that in the country I had done perhaps but little for the poor, the help which had been required of me was so small; but even the little I had done had been useful, and had formed round me an atmosphere of love and sympathy with my fellow-creatures, in the midst of whom it might yet be possible for me to quiet the gnawing of my conscience as to the unlawfulness of my life of luxury.

On going to the city I had hoped for the same happy relations with the poor, but here things were upon quite another footing. In the city, poverty was at once less truthful, more exacting, and more bitter, than in the country. It was chiefly because there was so much more of it accumulated together, that it produced upon me a most harrowing impression. What I experienced at Liapin's house made my own luxurious life seem monstrously evil. I could not doubt the sincerity and strength of this conviction; yet, notwithstanding this, I was quite incapable of carrying out a revolution which demanded an entire change in my mode of life: I was frightened at the prospect, and so I resorted to compromises. I accepted what I was told by everyone, and what has been said by everybody since the world began,—that riches and luxury are in themselves no evil, that they are given by God, and that whilst continuing to live luxuriously it is possible to help those in need. I believed this and wanted to do so. And I wrote an article in which I called upon all rich people to help. These all admitted themselves morally obliged to agree with me, but evidently did not wish to do or give anything for the poor, or could not do so.

I then began visiting, and discovered what I had in no way expected to see. On the one hand, I saw in these dens (as I had at first called them) men whom it was impossible for me to help, because they were working-men, accustomed to labour and privation, and therefore having a much firmer hold on life than I had. On the other hand, I saw miserable men whom I could not aid because they were just such as I was myself. The majority of the poor whom I saw were wretched, merely because they had lost the capacity, desire, and habit of earning their bread; in other words, their misery consisted in the fact that they were just like myself. Whereas, of poor people to whom it was possible to give immediate assistance—those suffering from illness, cold, and hunger,—I found none, except the starving Agafia; and I became persuaded that, being so far removed from the life of those whom I wished to succour, it was almost impossible to find such need as I sought, because all real need was attended to by those amongst whom these unhappy creatures lived: and my principal conviction now was, that, with money, I could never reform that life of misery which these people led.

I was persuaded of this: yet a feeling of shame to leave off all I had begun, and self-deception as to my own virtues, made me continue my plan for some time longer till it died a natural death; thus, only with great difficulty and the help of Iván Fedotitch, I managed to distribute in the tavern at Rzhanoff's house the thirty-seven rubles which I considered were not my own.

Of course I might have continued this style of thing and have transformed it into a kind of charity; and, by importuning those who promised to give me money, I might have obtained and distributed more, thus comforting myself with the idea of my own excellence: but I became convinced on the one hand that we rich people do not wish,—and are also unable,—to distribute to the poor a portion of our superfluities (we have so many wants ourselves), and that money should not be given to any one if we really wish to do good, instead of merely distributing it at random as I had done in the Rzhanoff tavern. So I dropped the affair entirely and in despair quitted Moscow for my own village.

I intended on returning home to write a pamphlet on my experience, and to state why my project had not succeeded. I wanted to justify myself from the imputations which resulted from my article on the census; I wanted also to denounce society and its heartless indifference; and I desired to point out the causes of this town misery, and the necessity for endeavouring to remedy it, as well as the means which I thought were requisite for this purpose. I began even then to write, and fancied I had many very important facts to communicate. But in vain did I rack my brain: I could not manage it, notwithstanding the super-abundance of material at my command, because of the irritation under which I wrote, and because I had not yet learned by experience what was necessary to grasp the question rightly; still more because I had not become fully conscious of the cause of it all,—a very simple cause, deep-rooted in myself. So the pamphlet was not finished at the commencement of the present year (1884–1885).

In the matter of moral law we witness a strange phenomenon to which men pay too little attention. If I speak to an unlearned man about geology, astronomy, history, natural philosophy, or mathematics, he receives the information as quite new to him, and never says to me, "There is nothing new in what you tell me; every one knows it, and I have known it for a long time." But tell a man one of the highest moral truths in the simplest manner, in such a way as it has never been before formulated, and every ordinary man, particularly one who does not take any interest in moral questions, and, above all, one who dislikes them, is sure to say, "Who does not know that? It has been always known and expressed." And he really believes this. Only those who can appreciate moral truths know how to value their elucidation and simplification by a long and laborious process, or can prize the transition from a proposition or desire at first vaguely understood to a firm and determined expression calling for a corresponding change of conduct.

We are all accustomed to consider moral doctrine to be a very insipid and dull affair in which there can be nothing new or interesting; whereas, in reality, human life, with all its complicated and varied actions which seem to have no connection with morals,— political activity, activity in the sciences, in the arts, and in commerce,—has no other object than to elucidate moral truths more and more, and to confirm, simplify, and make them accessible to all.

I recollect once while walking in a street in Moscow I saw a man come out and examine the flag-stones attentively; then, choosing one of them, he sat down by it and began to scrape and rub it vigorously.

"What is he doing with the pavement?" I wondered; and, having come up close to him, I discovered he was a young man from a butcher's shop, and was sharpening his knife on the flag-stone. He was not thinking about the stones when examining them, and still less while doing his work; he was merely sharpening his knife. It was necessary for him to do so in order to cut the meat, but to me it seemed that he was doing something to the pavement.

In the same way mankind seems to be occupied with commerce, treaties, wars, sciences, arts; and yet for them one thing only is important, and they do only that,— they are elucidating those moral laws by which they live.

Moral laws are already in existence, and mankind has been and is merely re-discovering them: this elucidation appears to be unimportant and imperceptible to one who has no need of moral law, and who does not desire to live by it. Yet this is not only the chief but is the sole business of all men. The elucidation is imperceptible in the same way as the difference between a sharp knife and a blunt one is imperceptible. A knife remains a knife; and one who has not to cut anything with it will not notice its edge: but for one who understands that all his life depends more or less upon whether his knife is blunt or sharp, every improvement in sharpening it is important; and such a man knows that there must be no limit to this improvement, and that the knife is only really a knife when it is sharp, and when it cuts what it has to cut.

The conviction of this truth flashed upon me when I began to write my pamphlet. Previously it seemed to me that I knew everything about my subject, that I had a thorough understanding of everything connected with those questions which had been awakened in me by the impressions made in Liapin's house and during the census; but when I tried to sum them up, and to put them on paper, it turned out that the knife would not cut, and had to be sharpened: so it is only now after three years that I feel my knife is sharp enough for me to cut out what I want. It is not that I have learned new things: my thoughts are still the same; but they were blunt formerly; they kept diverging in every direction; there was no edge to them; nor was anything brought, as it is now, to one central point, to one most simple and plain conclusion.

CHAPTER XIII

I recollect that during the whole time of my unsuccessful endeavours to help the unfortunate inhabitants of Moscow, I felt I was like a man trying to help others out of a bog, who was all the time stuck fast in it himself. Every effort made me feel the instability of the ground upon which I was standing. I felt that I myself was in this bog, but the acknowledgement did not help me to look more closely under my feet to find out the nature of the ground on which I stood: I kept looking for some external means to remedy the evil.

I felt my life was a bad one, and that people ought not to live so; yet I did not come to the most natural and obvious conclusion: that I must first reform my own mode of life before I could have any conception of how to reform others. And so I began at the wrong end, as it were. I was living in town, and wished to improve the lives of the men there; but I soon became convinced that I had no power to do so; and then I began to ponder over the *nature* of town life and town misery.

I said to myself over and over again, "What is this town life and town misery? And why, while living in town, am I unable to help the town poor?" The only reply I found was, that I was powerless to do anything for them, First, because there were too many collected together in one place; Secondly, because none of them were at all like those in the country. And again I asked myself, "Why are there so many here, and in what do they differ from the country poor?"

To both these questions the answer was the same. The poor are numerous in towns because all who have nothing to subsist on in the country are collected there round the rich; and their peculiarity is due to the fact that they have all come into the towns from the country to get a living. (If there are any town poor born there, whose fathers and grandfathers were town born, these in their turn originally came there to get a living.) But what are we to understand by the expression, "getting a living in town"? There is something strange in the expression; it sounds like a joke when we reflect on its meaning. How is it that from the country,—i.e., from places where there are woods, meadows, corn and cattle, where the earth yields the treasures of fertility—men come away, to get a living in a place where there are none of these advantages, but only stones and dust? What then, do the words, "getting a living in town," mean?

Such a phrase is constantly used, both by the employed and their employers, as if it were quite clear and intelligible. I remember now all the hundreds and thousands of town people living well or ill with whom I had spoken about their object in coming here; and all of them, without exception, told me they had quitted their villages "to get a living"; that "Moscow neither sows nor reaps, yet lives in wealth"; that in Moscow there is abundance of everything; and that, therefore, in Moscow one may get the money which is needed in the country for corn, cottages, horses, and the other essentials of life.

But, in fact, the country is the source of all wealth; there, only, are real riches,—corn, woods, horses, and everything necessary. Why go to towns, then, to get what is to be had in the country? And why should people carry away from the country into the towns the things that are necessary for country people,—flour, oats, horses, and cattle?

Hundreds of times I have spoken thus with peasants who live in towns; and from my talks with them, and from my own observations, it became clear to me that the accumulation of country people in our cities is partly *necessary*, because they could not otherwise earn their livelihood, and partly voluntary, because they are attracted by the temptations of a town life.

It is true that the circumstances of a peasant are such, that, in order to satisfy the pecuniary demands made on him in his village, he cannot do otherwise than sell that corn and cattle which he knows very well will be necessary for himself; and he is compelled, whether he will or not, to go to town to earn back what was his own. But it is also true that he is attracted to town by the charms of a comparatively easy way of getting money, and by the luxury of life there; and, under the pretext of earning his living, he goes there in order to have easier work and better food, to drink tea three times a day, to dress himself smartly, and even to get drunk and lead a dissolute life.

The cause is a simple one; for property passing from the hands of the agriculturalists into those of non-agriculturalists accumulates in towns. Observe towards autumn how much wealth is gathered together in the villages. Then come the demands of taxes, rents, recruiting; then the temptations of vodka, marriages, feasts, peddlers, and all sorts of other snares; so that in one way or other, this property, all in its various forms (sheep, calves, cows, horses, pigs, poultry, eggs, butter, hemp, flax, rye, oats, buckwheat, peas, hemp-seed, and flax-seed), passes into the hands of strangers, and is taken first to provincial towns, and thence to the capitals. A villager is compelled to dispose of all these things in order to satisfy the demands made upon him and the temptations offered him; and, having thus parted with his goods, he is left in want, and must follow where his wealth has been taken; and there he tries to earn back the money which is necessary for his most urgent needs at home; and so, being partly carried away by these temptations, he himself, along with others, makes use of the accumulated wealth.

Everywhere throughout Russia, and, I think, not only in Russia but all over the world, the same thing happens. The wealth of the country people who produce it passes into the hands of tradespeople, landowners, government officials, manufacturers. The men who receive this wealth want to enjoy it, and to enjoy it fully they must be in town.

In the country, in the first place, it is difficult for the rich to gratify all their desires, owing to the inhabitants being scattered: you do not find there the shops, banks, restaurants, theatres, and various kinds of public amusements.

Secondly, another of the chief pleasures procured by wealth,—vanity, the desire to astonish, to make a display before others,—cannot be gratified in the country for the same reason: its inhabitants being too scattered. There is no one in the country to appreciate luxury; there is no one to astonish. There you may have what you like to embellish your dwelling,—pictures, bronze statues, all sorts of carriages, and fine toilets,—but there is nobody to look at them or to envy you. The peasants do not understand the value of all this, and cannot make head or tail of it. Thirdly, luxury in the country is even disagreeable to a man who has a conscience, and is an anxiety to a timid person. One feels uneasy or ashamed at taking a milk bath, or in feeding puppies with milk, when there are children close by needing it; one feels the same in building pavilions and gardens among a people who live in cottages covered with stable litter, and who have no wood to burn.

There is no one in the village to prevent the stupid, uneducated peasants from spoiling our comforts.

Therefore, rich people gather together in towns, and settle near those who, in similar positions, have similar desires. In towns, the enjoyment of luxuries is carefully protected by a numerous police. The principal inhabitants of towns are government officials, round whom all the rich people, master-workmen, and artisans have settled. There, a rich man has only to think about a thing, and he can get it. It is also more agreeable for him to live there, because he can gratify his vanity; there are people with whom he may try to compete in luxury, whom he may astonish or eclipse. But it is especially pleasant for a wealthy man to live in town, because, where his country life was uncomfortable, and even somewhat incongruous because of his luxury, in town, on the contrary, it would be uncomfortable for him *not* to live splendidly, as his equals in wealth do. What seemed out of place there, appears indispensable here.

Rich people collect together in towns, and, under the protection of the authorities, enjoy peacefully all that has been brought there by the villagers. A countryman often cannot help going to town, where a ceaseless round of feasting is going on, where what has been procured from the peasants is being spent. He comes into the town to feed on those crumbs which fall from the tables of the rich; and partly by observing the careless, luxurious, and generally approved mode of living of these men, he begins to desire to order his own affairs in such a manner that he, too, may be able to work less and avail himself more of the labour of others. At last he decides to settle down in the neighbourhood of the wealthy, trying by every means in his power to get back from them what is necessary for him, and submitting to all the conditions which the rich enforce. These country people assist in gratifying all the fancies of the wealthy: they serve them in public baths, in taverns, as coachmen, and as prostitutes. They manufacture carriages, make toys and dresses, and little by little learn from their wealthy neighbours how to live like them, not by real labour, but by all sorts of tricks, squeezing out from others the money they have collected,—and so they become depraved, and are ruined.

It is then this same population, depraved by the wealth of towns, which forms that city misery which I wished to relieve, but could not.

Indeed, if one only reflects on the condition of these country folk coming to town to earn money to buy bread or to pay taxes, and who see everywhere thousands of rubles squandered foolishly, and hundreds very easily earned while they have to earn their pence by the hardest of labour, one cannot but be astonished that there are still many such people at work, and that they do not all have recourse to a more easy way of getting money,—trading, begging, vice, cheating, and even robbery.

It is only we who join in the ceaseless orgie going on in the towns who can get so accustomed to our own mode of life that it seems quite natural to us that one fine gentleman should occupy five large rooms heated with sufficient firewood to enable twenty families to warm their homes and cook their food with. To drive a short distance, we employ two thoroughbreds and two men; we cover our inlaid floors with carpets, and spend five or ten thousand rubles on a ball, or even twenty-five for a Christmas-tree, and so on. Yet a man who needs ten rubles to buy bread for his family, or from whom his last sheep has been taken to meet a tax of seven rubles which he cannot save by the hardest of labour, cannot get accustomed to all this which we imagine must seem quite natural to the poor. There are even people *naïve* enough to say that the poor are thankful to us because we feed them by living so luxuriously!

But poor people do not lose their reasoning powers because they are poor: they reason quite in the same manner as we do. When we have heard that some one has lost a fortune at cards, or squandered ten or twenty thousand rubles, the first thought that comes into our minds is: "How stupid and bad this man must be to have parted with such a large sum without any equivalent; and how well *I* could have employed this money for some building I have long wanted to get done, or for the improvement of my estate," and so on.

The poor reason in the same way on seeing how foolishly we waste our wealth; all the more forcibly, because this money is needed, not to satisfy their *whims*, but for the chief necessaries of life, of which they are in want. We are greatly mistaken in thinking that the poor, while able to reason thus, still look on unconcernedly at the luxury around them.

They have never acknowledged, and never will, that it is right for one man to be always idling, and for another to be continually working. At first they are astonished and offended; then, looking closer into the question, they see that this state of things is acknowledged to be legal, and they themselves try to get rid of work, and to take part in the feasting. Some succeed in so doing, and acquire similar wanton habits; others, little by little, approach such a condition; others break down before they reach their object, and, having lost the habit of working, fill the night-houses and the haunts of vice.

The year before last we took from the village a young peasant to be our butler's assistant. He could not agree with the footman, and was sent away; he entered the service of a merchant, pleased his masters, and now wears a watch and chain, and has smart boots.

In his place we took another peasant, a married man. He turned out a drunkard, and lost money. We took a third: he began to drink, and, having drunk all he had, was for a long time in distress in a night-lodging-house. Our old cook took to drinking in the town, and fell ill. Last year a footman who used formerly to have fits of drunkenness, but who, while living in the village kept himself from it for five years, came to live in Moscow without his wife (who used to keep him in order), began again to drink, and ruined himself. A young boy of our village is living as butler's assistant at my brother's. His grandfather, a blind old man, came to me while I was living in the country, and asked me to persuade this grandson to send ten rubles for taxes, because, unless this were done, the cow would have to be sold.

"He keeps telling me that he has to dress himself respectably," said the old man. "He got himself long boots, and that ought to be enough; but I actually believe he would like to buy a watch!"

In these words the grandfather expressed what he felt was the utmost degree of extravagance. And this was really so; for the old man could not afford a drop of oil for his food during the whole of Lent, and his wood was spoilt because he had not the ruble and a quarter necessary for cutting it up. But the old man's irony turned out to be reality. His grandson came to me dressed in a fine black overcoat, and in long boots for which he had paid eight rubles. Recently he had got ten rubles from my brother, and spent them on his boots. And my children, who have known the boy from his infancy, told me that he really considers it necessary to buy a watch. He is a very good boy, but he considers that he will be laughed at for not having one.

This year a housemaid, eighteen years of age, formed an intimacy with the coachman, and was sent away. Our old nurse, to whom I related the case, reminded me of a girl whom I had quite forgotten. Ten years ago, during a short stay in Moscow, she formed an intimacy with a footman. She also was sent away, and drifted at last into a house of ill-fame, and died in a hospital before she was twenty years of age.

We have only to look around us to become alarmed by the infection which (to say nothing of manufactories and workshops existing only to gratify our luxury) we directly, by our luxurious town life, spread among those very people whom we desire afterwards to help.

Thus, having got at the root of that town misery which I was not able to alleviate, I saw that its first cause is in our taking from the villagers their necessaries and carrying them to town. The second cause is, that in those towns we avail ourselves of what we have gathered from the country, and, by our foolish luxury, tempt and deprave the peasants who follow us there in order to get back something of what we have taken from them in the country.

CHAPTER XIV

From another point of view than the one stated, I also came to the same conclusion. Recollecting my connection with the town-poor during this period, I saw that one cause which prevented me from helping them was their insincerity and falseness. They all considered me, not as an individual but merely as a means to an end. I felt I could not become intimate with them; I thought I did not perhaps understand how to do so; but without truthfulness, no help was possible. How can one help a man who does not tell all his circumstances? Formerly I accused the poor of this (it is so natural to accuse others), but one word spoken by a remarkable man, Sutaief, who was then on a visit at my house, cleared up the difficulty, and showed me wherein lay the cause of my failure.

I remember that even then what he said made a deep impression on me; but I did not understand its full meaning until afterwards. It happened that while in the full ardour of my self-deception I was at my sister's house, Sutaief being also there; and my sister was questioning me about my work.

I was relating it to her; and, as is always the case when one does not fully believe in one's own enterprises, I related with great enthusiasm, ardour, and at full length, all I had been doing, and all the possible results. I was telling her how we should keep our eyes open to what went on in Moscow; how we should take care of orphans and old people; how we should afford means for impoverished villagers to return to their homes, and pave the way to reform the depraved. I explained, that, if we succeeded in our undertaking, there would not be in Moscow a single poor man who could not find help.

My sister sympathized with me; and while speaking, I kept looking now and then at Sutaief; knowing his Christian life, and the importance attached by him to works of charity, I expected sympathy from him, and I spoke so that he might understand me; for, though I was addressing my sister, yet my conversation was really more directed to him.

He sat immovable, dressed in his black-tanned-sheepskin coat, which he, like other peasants, wore in-doors as well as out. It seemed that he was not listening to us, but was thinking about something else. His small eyes gave no responding gleam, but seemed to be turned inwards. Having spoken out to my own satisfaction, I turned to him and asked him what he thought about it.

"The whole thing is worthless," he replied.

"Why?"

"The plan is an empty one, and no good will come of it," he repeated with conviction.

"But why will nothing come of it? Why is it a useless business, if we help thousands, or even hundreds, of unhappy ones? Is it a bad thing, according to the gospel, to clothe the naked, or to feed the hungry?"

"I know, I know; but what you are doing is not that. Is it possible to help thus? You are walking in the street; somebody asks you for a few kopeks; you give them to him. Is that charity? Do him some spiritual good; teach him. What you give him merely says, 'Leave me alone.'"

"No; but that is not what we were speaking of: we wish to become acquainted with the wants, and then to help by money and by deeds. We will try to find for the poor people some work to do."

"That would be no way of helping them."

"How then? must they be left to die of starvation and cold?"

"Why left to die? How many are there of them?"

"How many?" said I, thinking that he took the matter so lightly from not knowing the great number of these men; "you are not aware, I dare say, that there are in Moscow about twenty thousand cold and hungry. And then, think of those in St. Petersburg and other towns!"

He smiled.

"Twenty thousand! And how many households are there in Russia alone? Would they amount to a million?"

"Well; but what of that?"

"What of that?" said he, with animation, and his eyes sparkled. "Let us unite them with ourselves; I am not rich myself, but will at once take two of them. Here is a fellow you settled in your kitchen; I asked him to go with me, but he refused. If there were ten times as many, we should take them all into our families. You one, I another. We shall work together; he will see how I work; he will learn how to live, and we shall eat out of one bowl, at one table; and they will hear a good word from me, and from you also. That is charity; but all this plan of yours is no good."

These plain words made an impression upon me. I could not help recognizing that they were true. But it seemed to me then, that, notwithstanding the justice of what he said, my proposed plan might perhaps be useful also.

But the longer I was occupied with this affair; and the closer my intercourse with the poor, the oftener I recollected these words and the greater meaning I found in them.

I, indeed, go in an expensive fur coat, or drive in my own carriage to a man who is in want of boots: he sees my house which costs two hundred rubles a month, or he notices that I give away, without thinking, five rubles, only because of a caprice; he is then aware that if I give away rubles in such a manner, it is because I have accumulated so many that I have a lot to spare which I am not only never in the habit of giving to any one, but which I have taken away from others without compunction. What can he see in me but one of those persons who have become possessed of something which should belong to him? And what other feelings can he have towards me than the desire to get back as many as possible of these rubles which were taken by me from him and from others?

I should like to become intimate with him, and complain that he is not sincere. But I am afraid to sit down upon his bed for fear of lice or some infectious disease; I am also afraid to let him come into my room; and when he comes to me half-dressed, he has to wait, if fortunate, in the entrance-hall, but oftener in the cold porch. And then I say that it is all his fault that I cannot become intimate with him, and that he is not sincere.

Let the most hard-hearted man sit down to dine upon five courses among hungry people who have little or nothing to eat except dry bread, and no one could have the heart to eat while these hungry people are around him licking their lips.

Therefore, before one can eat well when living among half-starved men, the first thing necessary is to hide ourselves from them, and to eat so that they may not see us. This is the very thing we do in the first place.

I looked into our own mode of life without prejudice, and became aware that it was not by chance that closer intercourse with the poor is difficult for us, but that we ourselves are intentionally ordering our lives in such a way as to make this intercourse impossible. And not only this; but, on looking at our lives, or at the lives of rich people from without, I saw that all that is considered as the *happiness* of these lives consists in being separated as much as possible from the poor, or is in some way or other connected with this desired separation.

In fact, the entire aim of our lives, beginning with food, dress, dwelling and cleanliness, and ending with our education, consists in placing a gulf between us and them. And we spend nine-tenths of our wealth to erect impassable barriers in order to establish this distinction and separation.

The first thing a man who has grown rich does is to leave off eating with others out of one bowl. He arranges plates for himself and his family, and separates himself from the kitchen and the servants. He feeds his servants well so that their mouths may not water, and he dines alone. But eating alone is dull. He invents whatever he can to improve his food, embellish his table; and the very manner of taking food, as at dinner-parties, becomes a matter of vanity and pride. His manner of eating his food is a means of separating himself from other people. For a rich man it is out of the question to invite a poor person to his table. One must know how to hand a lady to table, how to bow, how to sit, to eat, to use a finger-bowl, all of which the rich alone know how to do.

The same holds good with dress.

If a rich man wore ordinary dress,—a jacket, a fur coat, felt shoes, leather boots, an undercoat, trousers, a shirt,—he would require very little to cover his body and protect it from cold; and, having two fur coats, he could not help giving one away to somebody who had none. But the wealthy man begins with wearing clothes which consist of many separate parts, of use only on particular occasions, and therefore of no use to a poor man. The man of fashion must have evening dress-coats, waistcoats, frock-coats, patent-leather shoes; his wife must have bodices, and dresses which, according to fashion, are made of many parts, high-heeled shoes, hunting and travelling jackets, and so on. All these articles can be useful only to people in a condition far removed from poverty.

And thus dressing also becomes a means of isolation. Fashions make their appearance, and are among the chief things which separate the rich man from the poor one.

The same thing shows itself more plainly still in our dwellings. In order that one person may occupy ten rooms we must manage so that he may not be seen by the people who are living by tens in one room.

The richer a man is, the more difficult it is to get at him; the more footmen there are between him and people not rich, the more impossible it is for him to receive a poor guest, to let him walk on his carpets and sit on his satin-covered chairs.

The same thing happens in travelling. A peasant who drives in a cart or on a carrier's sledge must be very hard-hearted if he refuses to give a pedestrian a lift; he has enough room, and can do it. But the richer the carriage is, the more impossible it is to put any one in it besides the owner. Some of the most elegant carriages are so narrow as to be termed "*egotists*."

The same thing applies to all the modes of living expressed by the word "cleanliness." Cleanliness! Who does not know human beings, especially women, who make a great virtue of cleanliness? Who does not know the various phrases of this cleanliness, which have no limit whatever when it is procured by the labour of others? Who among self-made men has not experienced in his own person the pains with which he carefully accustomed himself to this cleanliness, which illustrates the saying, "White hands are fond of another's labour"?

To-day cleanliness consists in changing one's shirt daily; to-morrow it will be changed twice a day. At first, one has to wash one's hands and neck every day, then one will have to wash one's feet every day, and afterwards it will be the whole body, and in peculiar methods. A clean table-cloth serves for two days, then it is changed every day, and afterwards two table-cloths a day are used. To-day the footman is required to have clean hands; to-morrow he must wear gloves, and clean gloves, and he must hand the letters on a clean tray.

There are no limits to this cleanliness, which is of no other use to anyone except to separate us, and to make our intercourse with others impossible while the cleanliness is obtained through the labour of others.

Not only so, but when I had deeply reflected upon this, I came to the conclusion that what we term education is a similar thing. Language cannot deceive: it gives the right name to everything. The common people call education fashionable dress, smart conversation, white hands, and a certain degree of cleanliness. Of such a man they say, when distinguishing him from others, that he is an educated man.

In a little higher circle men denote by education the same things, but add playing on the piano, the knowledge of French, good Russian spelling, and still greater cleanliness.

In the still higher circle education consists of all this, with the addition of English, and a diploma from a high educational establishment, and a still greater degree of cleanliness. But in all these shades, education is in substance quite the same.

It consists in those forms and various kinds of information which separate a man from his fellow-creatures. Its object is the same as that of cleanliness: to separate us from the crowd, in order that they, hungry and cold, may not see how we feast. But it is impossible to hide ourselves, and our efforts are seen through.

Thus I became aware that the reason why it was impossible for us rich men to help the town poor was nothing more or less than the impossibility of our having closer intercourse with them, and that this barrier we ourselves create by our whole life and by all the uses we make of our wealth. I became persuaded that between us rich men and the poor there stood, erected by ourselves, a barrier of cleanliness and education which arose out of our wealth; and that, in order to be able to help them, we have first to break down this barrier and to render possible the realization of the means suggested by Sutaief: to take the poor into our respective homes. And so, as I have already said at the beginning of this chapter, I came to the same conclusion from a different point of view from that to which the train of thought about town misery had led me; viz., the cause of it all lay in our wealth.

CHAPTER XV

I began again to analyze the matter from a third and purely personal point of view. Among the phenomena which particularly impressed me during my benevolent activity, there was one,—a very strange one,—which I could not understand for a long time.

Whenever I happened, in the street or at home, to give a poor person a trifling sum without entering into conversation with him, I saw on his face, or imagined I saw, an expression of pleasure and gratitude, and I myself experienced an agreeable feeling at this form of charity. I saw that I had done what was expected of me. But when I stopped and began to question the man about his past and present life, entering more or less into particulars, I felt it was impossible to give him 3 or 20 kopeks; and I always began to finger the money in my purse, and, not knowing how much to give, I always gave more under these circumstances; but, nevertheless, I saw that the poor man went away from me dissatisfied. When I entered into still closer intercourse with him, my doubts as to how much I should give increased; and, no matter what I gave, the recipient seemed more and more gloomy and dissatisfied.

As a general rule, it always happens that if, upon nearer acquaintance with the poor man I gave him three rubles or even more, I always saw gloominess, dissatisfaction, even anger depicted on his face; and sometimes, after having received from me ten rubles, he has left me without even thanking me, as if I had offended him.

In such cases I was always uncomfortable and ashamed, and felt myself guilty. When I watched the poor person during weeks, months, or years, helped him, expressed my views, and became intimate with him, then our intercourse became a torment, and I saw that the man despised me. And I felt that he was right in doing so. When in the street a beggar asks me, along with other passers-by, for three kopeks, and I give it him, then, in his estimation, I am a kind and good man who gives "one of the threads which go to make the shirt of a naked one": he expects nothing more than a thread, and, if I give it, he sincerely blesses me.

But if I stop and speak to him as man to man, show him that I wish to be more than a mere passer-by, and, if, as it often happened, he shed tears in relating his misfortune, then he sees in me not merely a chance helper, but that which I wish him to see,—a kind man. If I am a kind man, my kindness cannot stop at twenty kopeks, or at ten rubles, or ten thousand. One cannot be a slightly kind man. Let us suppose that I give him much; that I put him straight, dress him, and set him on his legs so that he can help himself; but, from some reason or other, either from an accident or his own weakness, he again loses the great-coat and clothing and money I gave him, he is again hungry and cold, and he again comes to me, why should I refuse him assistance? For if the cause of my benevolent activity was merely the attainment of some definite, material object, such as giving him so many rubles or a certain great-coat, then, having given them I could be easy in my mind; but the cause of my activity was not this: the cause of it was my desire to be a kind man—i.e., to see myself in everybody else. Everyone understands kindness in this way, and not otherwise.

Therefore if such a man should spend in drink all you gave him twenty times over, and be again hungry and cold, then, if you are a benevolent man, you cannot help giving him more money, you can never leave off doing so while you have more than he has; but if you draw back, you show that all you did before was done not because you are benevolent, but because you wish to appear so to others and to him. And it was because I had to back out of such cases, and to cease to give, and thus to disown the good, that I felt a painful sense of shame.

What was this feeling, then?

I had experienced it in Liapin's house and in the country, and when I happened to give money or anything else to the poor, and in my adventures among the town people. One case which occurred lately reminded me of it forcibly, and led me to discover its cause.

It happened in the country. I wanted twenty kopeks to give to a pilgrim. I sent my son to borrow it from somebody. He brought it to the man, and told me that he had borrowed it from the cook. Some days after, other pilgrims came, and I was again in need of twenty kopeks. I had a ruble. I recollected what I owed the cook, went into the kitchen, hoping that he would have some more coppers. I said,—

"I owe you twenty kopeks: here is a ruble."

I had not yet done speaking when the cook called to his wife from the adjoining room: "Parasha, take it," he said.

Thinking she had understood what I wanted, I gave her the ruble. I must tell you that the cook had been living at our house about a week, and I had seen his wife, but had never spoken to her. I merely wished to tell her to give me the change, when she briskly bowed herself over my hand and was about to kiss it, evidently thinking I was giving her the ruble. I stammered out something and left the kitchen. I felt ashamed, painfully ashamed, as I had not felt for a long time. I actually trembled, and felt that I was making a wry face; and, groaning with shame, I ran away from the kitchen.

This feeling, which I fancied I had not deserved, and which came over me quite unexpectedly, impressed me particularly, because it was so long since I had felt anything like it and also because I fancied that I, an old man, had been living in a way I had no reason to be ashamed of.

This surprised me greatly. I related the case to my family, to my acquaintances, and they all agreed that they also would have felt the same. And I began to reflect: Why is it that I felt so?

The answer came from a case which had formerly occurred to me in Moscow. I reflected upon this case, and I understood the shame which I felt concerning the incident with the cook's wife, and all the sensations of shame I had experienced during my charitable activity in Moscow, and which I always feel when I happen to give anything beyond trifling alms to beggars and pilgrims, which I am accustomed to give, and which I consider not as charity, but as politeness and good breeding. If a man asks you for a light, you must light a match if you have it. If a man begs for three or twenty kopeks, or a few rubles, you must give if you have them. It is a question of politeness, not of charity.

The following is the case I referred to. I have already spoken about the two peasants with whom I sawed wood three years ago. One Saturday evening, in the twilight, I was walking with them back to town. They were going to their master to receive their wages. On crossing the Dragomilor bridge we met an old man. He begged, and I gave him twenty kopeks. I gave, thinking what a good impression my alms would make upon Simon, with whom I had been speaking on religious questions.

Simon, the peasant from Vladímir, who had a wife and two children in Moscow, also stopped, turned up the lappet of his kaftan, and took out his purse; and, after having looked over his money, he picked out a three-kopek piece, gave it to the old man, and asked for two kopeks back. The old man showed him in his hand two three-kopek pieces and a single kopek. Simon looked at it, was about to take one kopek, but, changing his mind, took off his cap, crossed himself, and went away, leaving the old man the three-kopek piece.

I was acquainted with all Simon's pecuniary circumstances. He had neither house nor other property. When he gave the old man the three kopeks, he possessed six rubles and fifty kopeks, which he had been saving up, and this was all the capital he had.

My property amounted to about six hundred thousand rubles. I had a wife and children, so also had Simon. He was younger than I, and had not so many children; but his children were young, and two of mine were grown-up men, old enough to work, so that our circumstances, independently of our property, were alike, though even in this respect I was better off than he.

He gave three kopeks, I gave twenty. What was, then, the difference in our gifts? What should I have given in order to do as he had done? He had six hundred kopeks; out of these he gave one, and then another two. I had six hundred thousand rubles. In order to give as much as Simon gave, I ought to have given three thousand rubles, and asked the man to give me back two thousand; and, in the event of his not having change, to leave him these two also, cross myself, and go away calmly, conversing about how people live in the manufactories, and what is the price of liver in the Smolensk market.

I thought about it at the time, but it was long before I was able to draw from this case the conclusion which inevitably follows from it. This conclusion appears to be so uncommon and strange, notwithstanding its mathematical accuracy, that it requires time to get accustomed to it. One is inclined to think there is some mistake, but there is none. It is only the terrible darkness of prejudice in which we live.

This conclusion, when I arrived at it and recognized its inevitableness, explained to me the nature of my feelings of shame in the presence of the cook's wife, and before all the poor to whom I gave and still give money. Indeed, what is that money which I give to the poor, and which the cook's wife thought I was giving her? In the majority of cases it forms such a minute part of my income that it cannot be expressed in a fraction comprehensible to Simon or to a cook's wife,—it is in most cases a millionth part or thereabout. I give so little that my gift is not, and cannot be, a sacrifice to me: it is only a something with which I amuse myself when and how it pleases me. And this was indeed how my cook's wife had understood me. If I gave a stranger in the street a ruble or twenty kopeks, why should I not give her also a ruble? To her, such a distribution of money is the same thing as a gentleman throwing gingerbread nuts into a crowd. It is the amusement of people who possess much "fool's money." I was ashamed, because the mistake of the cook's wife showed me plainly what ideas she and all poor people must have of me. "He is throwing away 'fool's money'"; that is, money not earned by him.

And, indeed, what is my money, and how did I come by it? One part of it I collected in the shape of rent for my land, which I had inherited from my father. The peasant sold his last sheep or cow in order to pay it.

Another part of my money I received from the books I had written. If my books are harmful, and yet sell, they can only do so by some seductive attraction, and the money which I receive for them is badly earned money; but if my books are useful, the thing is still worse. I do not give them to people, but say, "Give me so many rubles, and I will sell them to you."

As in the former case a peasant sells his last sheep, here a poor student or a teacher does it: each poor person who buys denies himself some necessary thing in order to give me this money. And now that I have gathered much of such money what am I to do with it? I take it to town, give it to the poor only when they satisfy all my fancies and come to town to clean pavements, lamps, or boots, to work for me in the factories, and so on. And with this money I draw from them all I can. I try to give them as little as I can and take from them as much as possible.

Now, quite unexpectedly, I begin to share all this said money with these same poor persons for nothing; but not with everyone, only as fancy prompts me. And why should not every poor man expect that his turn might come to-day to be one of those with whom I amuse myself by giving them my "fool's money"?

So everyone regards me as the cook's wife did. And I had gone about with the notion that this was charity,—this taking away thousands with one hand, and with the other throwing kopeks to those I select!

No wonder I was ashamed. But before I can begin to do good I must leave off the evil and put myself in a position in which I should cease to cause it. But all my course of life is evil. If I were to give away a hundred thousand, I should not yet have put myself in a condition in which I could do good, because I have still five hundred thousand left.

It is only when I possess nothing at all that I shall be able to do a little good; such as, for instance, the poor prostitute did who nursed a sick woman and her child for three days. Yet this seemed to me to be but so little! And *I* ventured to think of doing good! One thing only was true, which I at first felt on seeing the hungry and cold people outside Liapin's house,—that *I* was guilty of that; and that to live as I did was impossible, utterly impossible. What shall we do then? If somebody still needs an answer to this question, I will, by God's permission, give one, in detail.

CHAPTER XVI

It was hard for me to own this; but when I had got so far I was terrified at the delusion in which I had been living. I had been head over ears in the mud myself, and yet I had been trying to drag others out of it.

What is it that I really want? I want to do good; I want to contrive so that no human beings shall be hungry and cold, and that men may live as it is proper for them to live. I desire this; and I see that in consequence of all sorts of violence, extortions, and various expedients in which I too take part, the working people are deprived of the necessary things, and the non-working community, to whom I also belong, monopolize the labour of others. I see that this use of other people's labour is distributed thus: That the more cunning and complicated the devices employed by the man himself (or by those from whom he has inherited his property), the more largely he employs the labours of other people, and the less he works himself.

First come the millionaires; then the wealthy bankers, merchants, land-owners, government officials; then the smaller bankers, merchants, government officials and land-owners, to whom I belong too; then shopmen, publicans, usurers, police sergeants and inspectors, teachers, sacristans, clerks; then, again, house-porters, footmen, coachmen, water-carters, cabmen, pedlers; and then, last of all, the workmen, factory hands and peasants, the number of this class in proportion to the former being as ten to one.

I see that the lives of nine-tenths of the working people essentially require exertion and labour, like every other natural mode of living; but that, in consequence of the devices by which the necessaries of life are taken away from these people, their lives become every year more difficult, and more beset with privations; and our lives, the lives of the non-labouring community, owing to the co-operation of sciences and arts which have this very end in view, become every year more sumptuous, more attractive and secure.

I see that in our days the life of a labouring man, and especially the lives of the old people, women, and children of the working-classes, are quite worn away by increased labour out of proportion to their nourishment, and that even the very first necessaries of life are not secured for them. I see that side by side with these the lives of the non-labouring class, to which I belong, are each year more and more filled up with superfluities and luxury, and are becoming continually more secure. The lives of the wealthy have reached that degree of security of which in olden times men only dreamed in fairy-tales, to the condition of the owner of the magic purse with the "inexhaustible ruble"; to a state where a man not only is entirely free from the law of labour for the sustenance of his life, but has the possibility of enjoying all the goods of this life without working, and of bequeathing to his children, or to anyone he chooses, this purse with the "inexhaustible ruble."

I see that the results of the labour of men pass over more than ever from the masses of labourers to those of the non-labourers; that the pyramid of the social structure is, as it were, being rebuilt, so that the stones of the foundation pass to the top, and the rapidity of this passage increases in a kind of geometric progression.

I see that there is going on something like what would take place in an ant-hill if the society of ants should lose the sense of the general law, and some of them were to take the results of labour out of the foundations and carry them to the top of the hill, making the foundation narrower and narrower and thus enlarging the top, and so by that means cause their fellows to pass also from the foundation to the top.

I see that instead of the ideal of a laborious life, men have created the ideal of the purse with the "inexhaustible ruble." The rich, I among their number, arrange this ruble for themselves by various devices; and in order to enjoy it we locate ourselves in towns, in a place where nothing is produced but everything is swallowed up.

The poor labouring man, swindled so that the rich may have this magic ruble, follows them to town; and there he also has recourse to tricks, either arranging matters so that he may work little and enjoy much (thus making the condition of other workingmen still more heavy), or, not having attained this state, he ruins himself and drifts into the continually and rapidly increasing number of cold and hungry tenants of doss-houses.

I belong to the class of those men who by means of these various devices take away from the working people the necessaries of life, and who thus, as it were, create for themselves the inexhaustible fairy ruble which tempts in turn these unfortunate ones.

I wish to help men; and therefore it is clear that first of all I ought on the one side to cease to plunder them as I am doing now, and on the other to leave off tempting them. But by means of most complicated, cunning, and wicked contrivances practised for centuries, I have made myself the owner of this ruble; that is, have got into a condition where, never doing anything myself, I can compel hundreds and thousands of people to work for me, and I am really availing myself of this privileged monopoly notwithstanding that all the time I imagine I pity these men and wish to help them.

I sit on the neck of a man, and having quite crushed him down compel him to carry me and will not alight from off his shoulders, though I assure myself and others that I am very sorry for him and wish to ease his condition by every means in my power—except by getting off his back.

Surely this is plain. If I wish to help the poor, that is, to make the poor cease to be poor, I ought not to create the poor. Yet I give money capriciously to those who have gone astray, and take away tens of rubles from men who have not yet become bad, thereby making them poor and at the same time depraved.

This is very clear; but it was exceedingly difficult for me to understand at first, without some modification or reserve which would justify my position. However as soon as I come to see my own error, all that formerly appeared strange, complicated, clouded, and inexplicable, became quite simple and intelligible; but the important matter was, that the direction of my life indicated by this explanation, became at once, simple, clear, and agreeable, instead of being, as formerly, intricate, incomprehensible, and painful.

Who am I, I thought, that desire to better men's condition? I say I desire this, and yet I do not get up till noon, after having played cards in a brilliantly lighted saloon all night,—I, an enfeebled and effeminate man requiring the help and services of hundreds of people, I come to help them! to help these men who rise at five, sleep on boards, feed on cabbage and bread, understand how to plough, to reap, to put a handle to an axe, to hew, to harness horses, to sew; men who, by their strength and perseverance and skill and self-restraint are a hundred times stronger than I who come to help them.

What *could* I experience in my intercourse with these people but shame? The weakest of them, a drunkard, an inhabitant of Rzhanoff's house, he whom they call "the sluggard," is a hundred times more laborious than I; his balance, so to say,—in other words the relation between what he takes from men and what he gives to them,—is a thousand times more to his credit than mine when I count what I receive from others and what I give them in return. And such men I go to assist!

I go to help the poor. But of the two who is the poorer? No one is poorer than myself. I am a weak, good-for-nothing parasite who can only exist under very peculiar conditions, can live only when thousands of people labour to support this life which is not useful to anyone. And I, this very caterpillar which eats up the leaves of a tree, I wish to help the growth and the health of the tree and to cure it!

All my life is spent thus: I eat, talk, and listen; then I eat, write, or read, which are only talking and listening in another form; I eat again, and play; then eat, talk, and listen, and finally eat and go to sleep: and thus every day is spent; I neither do anything else nor understand how to do it. And in order that I may enjoy this life it is necessary that from morning till night house-porters, dvorniks, cooks (male and female), footmen, coachmen, and laundresses, should work; to say nothing of the manual labour necessary so that the coachmen, cooks, footmen, and others may have the instruments and articles by which and upon which they work for me,—axes, casks, brushes, dishes, furniture, glasses, shoe-black, kerosene, hay, wood, and food. All these men and women work hard all the day and every day in order that I may talk, eat, and sleep. And I, this useless man, imagined I was able to benefit the very people who were serving me! That I did not benefit any one and that I was ashamed of myself, is not so strange as the fact that such a foolish idea ever came into my mind.

The woman who nursed the sick old man helped him; the peasant's wife, who cut a slice of her bread earned by herself, from the very sowing of the corn that made it, helped the hungry one; Simon, who gave three kopeks which he had earned, assisted the pilgrim, because these three kopeks really represented his labour; but I had served nobody, worked for no one, and knew very well that my money did not represent my labour.

And so I felt that in money, or in money's worth, and in the possession of it, there was something wrong and evil; that the money itself, and the fact of my having it, was one of the chief causes of those evils which I had seen before me; and I asked myself, What is money?

CHAPTER XVII

Money! Then what is money?

It is answered, money represents labour. I meet educated people who even assert that money represents labour performed by those who possess it. I confess that I myself formerly shared this opinion, although I did not very clearly understand it. But now it became necessary for me to learn thoroughly what money is.

In order to do so, I addressed myself to science. Science says that money in itself is neither unjust nor pernicious; that money is the natural result of the conditions of social life, and is indispensable, first, for convenience of exchange; secondly, as a measure of value; thirdly, for saving; and fourthly, for payments.

The fact that when I have in my pocket three rubles to spare, which I am not in need of, I have only to whistle and in every civilized town I can obtain a hundred people ready for these three rubles to do the worst, most disgusting, and humiliating act I require, it is said, comes not from money, but from the very complicated conditions of the economical life of nations!

The dominion of one man over others does not come from money, but from the circumstance that a workingman does not receive the full value of his labour; and the fact that he does not get the full value of his labour depends upon the nature of capital, rent, and wages, and upon complicated connections between the distribution and consumption of wealth.

In plain language, it means that people who have money may twist round their finger those who have none. But science says that this is an illusion; that in every kind of production three factors take part,—land, savings of labour (capital), and labour, and that the dominion of the few over the many proceeds from the various connections between these factors of production, because the two first factors, land and capital, are not in the hands of working people; and from this fact and from the various combinations which result from it this domination proceeds.

Whence comes the great power of money, which strikes us all with a sense of its injustice and cruelty? Why is one man, by the means of money, to have dominion over others? Science says, "It comes from the division of the factors of production, and from the consequent combinations which oppress the worker."

This answer has always appeared to me to be strange, not only because it leaves one part of the question unnoticed (namely, the significance of money), but also because of the division of the factors of production, which to an unprejudiced man will always appear artificial and out of touch with reality. Science asserts that in every production three agents come into operation,—land, capital and labour; and along with this division it is understood that property (or its value in money) is naturally divided among those who possess one of these agents; thus, rent (the value of the ground) belongs to the land-owner; interest belongs to the capitalist; and wages to the worker.

Is this really so?

First, is it true that in every production only three agencies operate? Now, while I am writing proceeds the production of hay around me. Of what is this production composed? I am told of the land which produces the grass; of capital (scythes, rakes, pitch-forks, carts which are necessary for the housing of the hay); and of labour. But I see that this is not true. Besides the land, there is the sun and rain; and, in addition, social order, which has been keeping these meadows from any damage which might be caused by letting stray cattle graze upon them, the skill of workmen, their knowledge of language, and many other agencies of production,—which, for some unknown reason, are not taken into consideration by political economy.

The power of the sun is as necessary as the land, even more. I may mention the instances when men (in a town, for example), assume the right to keep out the sun from others by means of walls or trees. Why, then, is the sun not included among the factors of production?

Rain is another means as necessary as the ground itself. The air too. I can imagine men without water and pure air because other men had assumed to themselves the right to monopolise these essential necessaries of all. Public security is likewise a necessary element. Food and dress for workmen are similar factors in production; this is even recognized by some economists. Education, the knowledge of language which creates the possibility to apply work, is likewise an agent. I could fill a volume by enumerating such combinations, not mentioned by science.

Why, then, are three only to be chosen, and laid as a foundation for the science of political economy? Sunshine and water equally with the earth are factors in production, so with the food and clothes of the workers, and the transmission of knowledge. All may be taken as distinct factors in production. Simply because the right of men to enjoy the rays of the sun, rain, food, language, and audience, are challenged only on rare occasions; but the use of land and of the instruments of labour are constantly challenged in society.

This is the true foundation; and the division of the factors of production into three, is quite arbitrary, and is not involved in the nature of things. But it may perhaps be urged that this division is so suitable to man, that wherever economic relationships are formed these three factors appear at once and alone.

Let us see whether this is really so.

First of all, I look at what is around me,—at Russian colonists, of whom millions have for ages existed. They come to a land, settle themselves on it, and begin to work; and it does not enter the mind of any of them that a man who does not use the land can have any claim to it,—and the land does not assert any rights of its own. On the contrary, the colonists conscientiously recognize the communism of the land and the right of every one of them to plough and to mow wherever he likes.

For cultivation, for gardening, for building houses, the colonists obtain various implements of labour: nor does it enter the mind of any of them that these instruments of labour may be allowed to bring profit in themselves, and the capital does not assert any rights of its own. On the contrary, the colonists consciously recognize among themselves that all interest for tools, or borrowed corn or capital, is unjust.

They work upon a free land, labour with their own tools, or with those borrowed without interest, each for himself, or all together, for common business; and in such a community, it is impossible to prove either the existence of rent, interest accruing from capital, or remuneration for labour.

In referring to such a community I am not indulging my fancy but describing what has always taken place, not only among Russian colonists, but everywhere, as long as human nature is not sinned against.

I am describing what appears to everyone to be natural and rational. Men settle on land, and each member undertakes the business which suits him, and, having procured the necessary tools, does his own work.

If these men find it more convenient to work together, they form a workmen's association. But neither in separate households, nor in associations, will separate agents of production appear till men artificially and forcibly divide them. There will be simply labour and the necessary conditions of labour,—the sun which warms all, the air which they breathe, water which they drink, land on which they labour, clothes on the body, food in the stomach, stakes, shovels, ploughs, machines with which they work. And it is evident that neither the rays of the sun, nor the clothes on the body, nor the stakes, nor the spade, nor the plough, with which each man works, nor the machines with which they labour in the workmen's association, can belong to anyone else than those who enjoy the rays of the sun, breathe the air, drink the water, eat the bread, clothe their bodies, and labour with the spade or with the machines, because all these are necessary only for those who use them. And when men act thus, we see they act rationally.

Therefore, observing all the economic conditions created among men, I do not see that division into three is natural. I see, on the contrary, that it is neither natural nor rational.

But perhaps the setting apart of these three does not occur in primitive societies, only when the population increases and cultivation begins to develop it is unavoidable. And we cannot but recognise the fact that this division has occurred in European society.

Let us see whether it is really so.

We are told that in European society this division of agencies has been; that is, that one man possesses land, another accomplished the instruments of labour, and the third is without land and instruments.

We have grown so accustomed to this assertion that we are no longer struck by the strangeness of it. But in this assertion lies an inner contradiction. The conception of a labouring man, includes the land on which he lives and the tools with which he works. If he did not live on the land and had no tools he would not be a labourer. A workman deprived of land and tools never existed and never can exist. There cannot be a bootmaker without a house for his work built on land, without water, air, and tools to work with.

If the peasant has no land, horse, water or scythe; if the bootmaker is without a house, water, or awl, then that means that some one has driven him from the ground, or taken it from him, and has cheated him out of his scythe, cart, horse, or awl; but it does not in any way mean that there can be country labourers without scythes or bootmakers without tools.

As you cannot think of a fisherman on dry land without fishing implements, unless you imagine him driven away from the water by some one who has taken his fishing implements from him; so also you cannot picture a workman without land on which to live, and without tools for his trade, unless somebody has driven him from the former, or robbed him of the latter.

There may be men who are hunted from one place to another, and who, having been robbed, are compelled perforce to work for another man and make things necessary for themselves, but this does not mean that such is the nature of production. It means only that in such case, the natural conditions of production are violated.

But if we are to consider as factors of production all of which a workman may be deprived by force, why not count among these the claim on the person of a slave? Why not count claims on the rain and the rays of the sun?

One man might build a wall and so keep the sun from his neighbour; another might come who would turn the course of a river through his own pond and so contaminate its water; or claim a fellow-being as his own property. But none of these claims, although enforced by violence, can be recognised as a basis. It is therefore as wrong to accept the artificial rights to land and tools as separate factors in production, as to recognise as such the invented rights to use sunshine, air, water, or the person of another.

There may be men who claim the land and the tools of a workman, as there were men who claimed the persons of others, and as there may be men who assert their rights to the exclusive use of the rays of the sun, or of water and air. There may be men who drive away a workman from place to place, taking from him by force the products of his labour as they are produced, and the very instruments of its production, who compel him to work, not for himself, but for his master, as in the factories;—all this is possible; but the conception of a workman without land and tools is still an impossibility, as much as that a man can willingly become the property of another, notwithstanding men have claimed other men for many generations.

And as the claim of property in the person of another cannot deprive a slave of his innate right to seek his own welfare and not that of his master; so, too, the claim to the exclusive possession of land and the tools of others cannot deprive the labourer of his inherent rights as a man to live on the land and to work with his own tools, or with communal tools, as he thinks most useful for himself.

All that science can say in examining the present economic question, is this: that in Europe certain claims to the land and the tools of workmen are made, in consequence of which, for some of these workmen (but by no means for all of them), the proper conditions of production are violated, so that they are deprived of land and implements of labour and compelled to work with the tools of others. But it is certainly not established that this accidental violation of the law of production is the fundamental law itself.

In saying that this separate consideration of the factors is the fundamental law of production, the economist is doing the very thing a zoölogist would do, if on seeing a great many siskins with their wings cut, and kept in little cages, he should assert that this was the essential condition of the life of birds, and that their life is composed of such conditions.

However many siskins there may be, kept in paste-board houses, with their wings cut, a zoölogist cannot say that these, and a tiny pail of water running up rails, are the conditions of the birds' lives. And however great the number of workpeople there may be, driven from place to place, and deprived of their productions as well as their tools, the natural right of man to live on the land, and to work with his own tools, is essential to him, and so it will remain forever.

Of course there are some who lay claim to the land and to the tools of workmen, just as in former ages there were some who laid claim to the persons of others; but there can be no real division of men into lords and slaves—as they wanted to establish in the ancient world—any more than there can be any real division in the agents of production (land and capital, etc.), as the economists are trying to establish.

These unlawful claims on the liberty of other men, science calls "the natural conditions of production." Instead of taking its fundamental principles from the natural properties of human societies, science took them from a special case; and desiring to justify this case, it recognized the right of some men to the land on which other men earn their living, and to the tools with which others again work; in other words, it recognized as a right something which had never existed, and cannot exist, and which is in itself a contradiction, because the claim of the man to the land on which he does not labour, is in essence nothing else than the right to use the land which he does not use; the claim on the tools of others is nothing else than the assumption of a right to work with implements with which a man does not work.

Science, by dividing the factors of production, declares that the natural condition of a workman—that is, of a man in the true sense of the word—is the unnatural condition in which he lives at present, just as in ancient times, by the division of men into citizens and slaves, it was asserted that the unnatural condition of slavery was the natural condition of life.

This very division, which science has accepted only for the purpose of justifying the existing injustice, and the recognition of this division as the foundation of all its inquiries, is responsible for the fact that science vainly tries to explain existing phenomena and, denying the clearest and plainest answers to the questions that arise, gives answers which have absolutely no meaning in them.

The question of economic science is this: What is the cause of the fact that some men, by means of money, acquire an imaginary right to land and capital, and may make slaves of those who have no money? The answer which presents itself to common sense is, that it is the result of money, the nature of which is to enslave men.

But economic science denies this, and says: This arises, not from the nature of money, but from the fact that some men have land and capital, and others have neither.

We ask: Why do persons who possess land and capital oppress those who possess neither? And we are answered: Because they possess land and capital.

But this is just what we are inquiring about. Is not deprivation of land and tools enforced slavery? And the answer is like saying, "A remedy is narcotic because its effects are narcotic." Life does not cease to put this essential question, and even science herself notices and tries to answer it, but does not succeed, because, starting from her own fundamental principles, she only turns herself round in a vicious circle.

In order to give itself a satisfactory answer to the question, science must first of all deny that wrong division of the agents of production, and cease to acknowledge the result of the phenomena as being their cause; and she must seek, first the more obvious, and then the remoter, causes of those phenomena which constitute the matter questioned.

Science must answer the question, Why are some men deprived of land and tools while others possess both? or, Why is it that lands and tools are taken from the people who labour on the land and work with the tools?

And as soon as economic science puts this question to herself she will get new ideas which will transform all the previous ideas of sham science,—which has been moving in an unalterable circle of propositions,—that the miserable condition of the workers proceeds from the fact that they are miserable.

To simple-minded persons it must seem unquestionable that the obvious reason of the oppression of some men by others is money. But science, denying this, says that money is only a medium of exchange, which has no connection with slavery of men.

Let us see whether it is so or not.

CHAPTER XVIII

What is the origin of money? What are the conditions under which nations always have money, and under what circumstances need nations not use money?

There are small tribes in Africa, and one in Australia, who live as the Sknepies and the Drevlyans lived in olden times. These tribes lived by breeding cattle and cultivating gardens. We become acquainted with them at the dawn of history, and history begins by recording the fact that some invaders appear on the scene. And invaders always do the same thing: they take away from the aborigines everything they can take,—cattle, corn, and cloth; they even make prisoners, male and female, and carry them away.

In a few years the invaders appear again, but the people have not yet got over the consequences of their first misfortunes, and there is scarcely anything to take from them; so the invaders invent new and better means of making use of their victims.

These methods are very simple, and present themselves naturally to the mind of all men. The *first* is personal slavery. There is a drawback to this, because the invaders must take over the entire control and administration of the tribe, and feed all the slaves; hence, naturally, there appears the *second*. The people are left on their own land, but this becomes the recognized property of the invaders, who portion it out among the leading military men, by whose means the labour of the tribe is utilized and transferred to the conquerors.

But this, too, has its drawback. It is inconvenient to have to oversee all the production of the conquered people, and thus the *third* means is introduced, as primitive as the two former; this is, the levying of a certain obligatory tax to be paid by the conquered at stated periods.

The object of conquest is to take from the conquered the greatest possible amount of the product of their labour. It is evident, that, in order to do this, the conquerors must take the articles which are the most valuable to the conquered, and which at the same time are not cumbersome, and are convenient for keeping,—skins of animals, and gold.

So the conquerors lay upon the family or the tribe a tax in these skins or gold, to be paid at fixed times; and thus, by means of this tribute, they utilize the labour of the conquered people in the most convenient way.

When the skins and the gold have been taken from the original owners, they are compelled to sell all they have amongst themselves to obtain more gold and skins for their masters; that is, they have to sell their property and their labour.

So it was in ancient times, in the Middle Ages, and so it occurs now. In the ancient world, where the subjugation of one people by another was frequent, personal slavery was the most widespread method of subjugation, and the centre of gravity in this compulsion, owing to the non-recognition of the equality of men. In the Middle Ages, feudalism—land-ownership and the servitude connected with it—partly takes the place of personal slavery, and the centre of compulsion is transferred from persons to land. In modern times, since the discovery of America, the development of commerce, and the influx of gold (which is accepted as a universal medium of exchange), the money tribute has become, with the increase of state power, the chief instrument for enslaving men, and upon this all economic relations are now based.

In "The Literary Miscellany" there is an article by Professor Yanjoul in which he describes the recent history of the Fiji Islands. If I were trying to find the most pointed illustration of how in our day the compulsory money payment became the chief instrument in enslaving some men by others, I could not imagine anything more striking and convincing than this trustworthy history,—history based upon documents of facts which are of recent occurrence.

In the South-Sea Islands, in Polynesia, lives a race called the Fiji. The group on which they live, says Professor Yanjoul, is composed of small islands, which altogether comprise about forty thousand square miles. Only half of these islands are inhabited, by a hundred and fifty thousand natives and fifteen hundred white men. The natives were reclaimed from savagery a long time ago, and were distinguished among the other natives of Polynesia by their intellectual capacities. They appear to be capable of labour and development, which they proved by the fact that within a short period they became good workmen and cattle breeders.

The inhabitants were well-to-do, but in the year 1859 the condition of their state became desperate: the nation and its representative, Kakabo, were in need of money. This money, forty-five thousand dollars, was wanted as compensation or indemnification demanded of them by the United States of America for violence said to have been done by Fijis to some citizens of the American Republic.

To collect this, the Americans sent a squadron, which unexpectedly seized some of the best islands under the pretext of guaranty, and threatened to bombard and ruin the towns if the indemnification were not paid over on a certain date to the representatives of America.

The Americans were among the first colonists who came to the Fiji Islands with the missionaries. They chose and (under one pretext or another) took possession of the best pieces of land on the islands, and established there cotton and coffee plantations. They hired whole crowds of natives, binding them by contracts unknown to this half-civilized race, or they acted through special contractors and dealers of human merchandise.

Misunderstandings between these master planters and the natives, whom they considered almost as slaves, were unavoidable, and it was some of these quarrels which served as a pretext for the American indemnification.

Notwithstanding their prosperity the Fijis had preserved almost up to that time the forms of the so-called natural economy which existed in Europe during the Middle Ages: money was scarcely in circulation among them, and their trade was almost exclusively on the barter basis,—one merchandise being exchanged for another, and the few social taxes and those of the state being paid in rural products. What could the Fijis and their King Kakabo do, when the Americans demanded forty-five thousand dollars under terrible threats in the event of nonpayment? To the Fijis the very figures seemed inconceivable, to say nothing of the money itself, which they had never seen in such large quantities. After deliberating with other chiefs, Kakabo made up his mind to apply to the Queen of England, at first merely asking her to take the islands under her protection, but afterwards requesting definite annexation.

But the English regarded this request cautiously, and were in no hurry to assist the half-savage monarch out of his difficulty. Instead of giving a direct answer, they sent special commissioners to make inquiries about the Fiji Islands in 1860, in order to be able to decide whether it was worth while to annex them to the British Possessions, and to lay out money to satisfy the American claims.

Meanwhile the American Government continued to insist upon payment, and as a pledge held in their *de facto* dominion some of the best parts, and, having looked closely into the national wealth, raised their former claim to ninety thousand dollars, threatening to increase it still more if Kakabo did not pay at once.

Being thus pushed on every side, and knowing nothing of European means of credit accommodation, the poor king, acting on the advice of European colonists, began to try to raise money in Melbourne among the merchants, cost what it might, if even he should be obliged to yield his kingdom into private hands.

So in consequence of his application a commercial society was formed in Melbourne. This joint-stock company, which took the name of the "Polynesian Company," formed a treaty with the chiefs of the Fiji-Islanders on the most advantageous terms. It took over the debt to the American Government, pledging itself to pay it by several instalments; and for this the company received, according to the first treaty, one, and then two hundred thousand acres of the best land, selected by itself; perpetual immunity from all taxes and dues for all its factories, operations, and colonies, and the exclusive right for a long period to establish banks in the Fiji Islands, with the privilege of issuing unlimited notes.

This treaty was definitely concluded in the year 1868, and there has appeared in the Fiji Islands, side by side with the local government, of which Kakabo is the head, another powerful authority,—a commercial organization, with large estates over all the islands, exercising a powerful influence upon the government.

Up to this time the wants of the government of Kakabo had been satisfied with a payment in local products, and a small custom tax on goods imported. But with the conclusion of the treaty and the formation of the influential "Polynesian Company," the king's financial circumstances had changed.

A considerable part of the best land in his dominion having passed into the hands of the company, his income from the land had therefore diminished; on the other hand the income from the custom taxes also diminished, because the company had obtained for itself the right to import and export all kinds of goods free of duties.

The natives—ninety-nine per cent. of the population—had never paid much in custom duties, as they bought scarcely any of the European productions except some stuffs and hardware; and now, from the freeing of custom duties of many well-to-do Europeans along with the Polynesian Company, the income of King Kakabo was reduced to *nil*, and he was obliged to take steps to resuscitate it if possible.

He began to consult his white friends as to the best way to remedy the trouble, and they advised him to create the first direct tax in the country; and, in order, I suppose, to have less trouble about it, to make it in money. The tax was established in the form of a general poll-tax, amounting to one pound for every man, and to four shillings for every woman, throughout the islands.

As I have already said, there still exists on the Fiji Islands a natural economy and a trade by barter. Very few natives possess money. Their wealth consists chiefly of raw products and cattle; whilst the new tax required the possession of considerable sums of money at fixed times.

Up to that date a native had not been accustomed to any individual burden in the interests of his government, except personal obligations; all the taxes which had to be paid, were paid by the community or village to which he belonged, and from the common fields from which he received his principal income.

One alternative was left to him,—to try to raise money from the European colonists; that is, to address himself either to the merchant or to the planter.

To the first he was obliged to sell his productions on the merchant's own terms (because the tax-collector required money at a certain fixed date), or even to raise money by the sale of his expected harvest, which enabled the merchant to take iniquitous interest. Or he had to address himself to the planter, and sell him his labour; that is, to become his workman: but the wages on the Fiji Islands were very low (owing, I suppose, to the exceptionally great supply of labour); not exceeding a shilling a week for a grown-up man, or two pounds twelve shillings a year; and therefore, merely to be able to get the money necessary to pay his own tax, to say nothing of his family, a Fiji had to leave his house, his family, and his own land, often to go far away to another island, and enslave himself to the planter for at least half a year; even then there was the payment for his family, which he must provide by some other means.

We can understand the result of such a state of affairs. From his hundred and fifty thousand subjects, Kakabo collected only six thousand pounds; and so there began a forcible extortion of taxes, unknown till then, and a whole series of coercive measures.

The local administration, formerly incorruptible, soon made common cause with the European planters, who began to have their own way with the country. For nonpayment of the taxes the Fijis were summoned to the court, and sentenced not only to pay the expenses but also to imprisonment for not less than six months. The prison really meant the plantations of the first white man who chose to pay the tax-money and the legal expenses of the offender. Thus the white settlers received cheap labour to any amount.

At first this compulsory labour was fixed for not longer than half a year; but afterwards the bribed judges found it possible to pass sentence for eighteen months, and even then to renew the sentence.

Very quickly, in the course of a few years, the picture of the social condition of the inhabitants of Fiji was quite changed.

Whole districts, formerly flourishing, lost half of their population, and were greatly impoverished. All the male population, except the old and infirm, worked far away from their homes for European planters, to get money necessary for the taxes, or in consequence of the law court. The women on the Fiji Islands had scarcely ever worked in the fields, so that in the absence of the men, all the local farming was neglected and went to ruin. And in the course of a few years, half the population of Fiji had become the slaves of the colonists.

To relieve their position the Fiji-Islanders again appealed to England. A new petition was got up, subscribed by many eminent persons and chiefs, praying to be annexed to England; and this was handed to the British consul. Meanwhile, England, thanks to her scientific expeditions, had time not only to investigate the affairs of the islands, but even to survey them, and duly to appreciate the natural riches of this fine corner of the globe.

Owing to all these circumstances, the negotiations this time were crowned with full success; and in 1874, to the great dissatisfaction of the American planters, England officially took possession of the Fiji Islands, and added them to its colonies. Kakabo died, his heirs had a small pension assigned to them, and the administration of the islands was intrusted to Sir Hercules Robinson, the Governor of New South Wales. In the first year of its annexation the Fiji-Islanders had no self-government, but were under the direction of Sir Hercules Robinson, who appointed an administrator.

Taking the islands into their hands, the English Government had to undertake the difficult task of gratifying various expectations raised by them. The natives, of course, first of all expected the abolition of the hated poll-tax; one part of the white colonists (the Americans) looked with suspicion upon the British rule; and another part (those of English origin) expected all kinds of confirmations of their power over the natives,—

permission to enclose the land, and so on. The English Government, however, proved itself equal to the task; and its first act was to abolish for ever the poll-tax, which had created the slavery of the natives in the interest of a few colonists.

But here Sir Hercules Robinson had at once to face a difficult dilemma. It was necessary to abolish the poll-tax, which had made the Fijis seek the help of the English Government; but, at the same time, according to English colonial policy, the colonies had to support themselves; they had to find their own means for covering the expenses of the government. With the abolition of the poll-tax, all the incomes of the Fijis (from custom duties) did not amount to more than six thousand pounds, while the government expenses required at least seventy thousand a year.

Having abolished the money tax, Sir Hercules Robinson now thought of a labour tax; but this did not yield the sum necessary to feed him and his assistants. Matters did not mend until a new governor had been appointed,—Gordon,—who, to get out of the inhabitants the money necessary to keep him and his officials, resolved not to demand money until it had come sufficiently into general circulation on the islands, but to take from the natives their products, and to sell them himself.

This tragical episode in the lives of the Fijis is the clearest and best proof of the nature and true meaning of money in our time.

In this illustration every essential is represented. The first fundamental condition of slavery,—the guns, threats, murders, and plunder,—and lastly, money, the means of subjugation which has supplanted all the others. That which in an historical sketch of economical development, has to be investigated during centuries, we have here, where all the forms of monetary violence have fully developed themselves, concentrated in a space of ten years.

The drama begins thus: the American Government sends ships with loaded guns to the shores of the islands, whose inhabitants they want to enslave. The pretext of this threat is monetary; but the beginning of the tragedy is the levelling of guns against all the inhabitants,—women, children, old people, and men,—though innocent of any crime. "Your money or your life,"—forty-five thousand dollars, then ninety thousand or slaughter. But the ninety thousand are not to be had. So now begins the second act: it is the postponement of a measure which would be bloody, terrible, and concentrated in a short period; and the substitution of a suffering less perceptible, which can be laid upon all, and will last longer. And the natives, with their representative, seek to substitute for the massacre a slavery of money. They borrow money, and the method at once begins to operate like a disciplined army. In five years the thing is done,—the men have not only lost their right to utilize their own land and their property, but also their liberty,—they have become slaves.

Here begins act three. The situation is too painful, and the unfortunate ones are told they may change their master and become the slaves of another. Of freedom from the slavery brought about by the means of money there is not one thought. And the people call for another master, to whom they give themselves up, asking him to improve their condition. The English come, see that dominion over these islanders will give them the possibility of feeding their already too greatly multiplied parasites, and take possession of the islands and their inhabitants.

But it does not take them in the form of personal slaves, it does not take even the land, nor distribute it among its assistants. These old ways are not necessary now: only one thing is necessary,—taxes which must be large enough on the one hand to prevent the workingmen from freeing themselves from virtual slavery, and on the other hand, to feed luxuriously a great number of parasites. The inhabitants must pay seventy thousand pounds sterling annually,—that is the fundamental condition upon which England consents to free the Fijis from the American despotism, and this is just what was wanting for the final enslaving of the inhabitants. But it turns out that the Fiji-Islanders cannot under any circumstances pay these seventy thousand pounds in their present state. The claim is too great.

The English temporarily modify it, and take a part of it out in natural products in order that in time, when money has come into circulation, they may receive the full sum. They do not behave like the former company, whose conduct we may liken to the first coming of savage invaders into an uncivilized land, when they want only to take as much as possible and then decamp; but England behaves like a more clear-sighted enslaver; she does not kill at one blow the goose with the golden eggs, but feeds her in order that she may continue to lay them. England at first relaxes the reins for her own interest that she may hold them tight forever afterwards, and so has brought the Fiji-Islanders into that state of permanent monetary thraldom in which all civilized European people now exist, and from which their chance of escape is not apparent.

This phenomenon repeats itself in America, in China, in Central Asia; and it is the same in the history of the conquest of all nations.

Money is an inoffensive means of exchange when it is not collected while loaded guns are directed from the sea-shore against the defenceless inhabitants. As soon as it is taken by the force of guns, the same thing must inevitably take place which occurred on the Fiji Islands, and has always and everywhere repeated itself.

Men who consider it their lawful right to utilize the labour of others, will achieve their ends by the means of a forcible demand of a sum of money which will compel the oppressed to become the slaves of the oppressors.

Moreover, that will happen which occurred between the English and the Fijis,—the extortioners will always, in their demand for money, rather exceed the limit to which the amount of the sum required must rise, so that the enslaving may be earlier. They will respect this limit only while they have moral sense and sufficient money for themselves: they will overstep it when they lose their moral sense or even do not require funds.

As for governments, they will always exceed this limit,—first, because for a government there exists no moral sense of justice; and secondly, because, as everyone knows, every government is always in the greatest want of money, through wars and the necessity of giving gratuities to their allies. All governments are insolvent, and involuntarily follow a maxim expressed by a Russian statesman of the eighteenth century,—that the peasant must be sheared of his wool lest it grow too long. All governments are hopelessly in debt, and this debt on an average (not taking in consideration its occasional diminution in England and America) is growing at a terrible rate. So also grow the budgets; that is, the necessity of struggling with other extortioners, and of giving presents to those who assist in extortion, and because of that grows the land rent.

Wages do not increase, not because of the law of rent, but because taxes, collected with violence, exist, with the object of taking away from men their superfluities, so that they may be compelled to sell their labour to satisfy them,—utilizing their labour being the aim of raising the taxes.

And their labour can only be utilized when, on a general average, the taxes required are more than the labourers are able to give without depriving themselves of all means of subsistence. The increase of wages would put an end to the possibility of slavery; and therefore, as long as violence exists, wages can never be increased. The simple and plain mode of action of some men towards others, political economists term *the iron law*; the instrument by which such action is performed, they call a medium of exchange; and money is this inoffensive medium of exchange necessary for men in their transactions with each other.

Why is it, then, that, whenever there is no violent demand for money taxes, money in its true signification has never existed, and never can exist; but, as among the Fiji-Islanders, the Phœnicians, the Kirghis, and generally among men who do not pay taxes, such as the Africans, there is either a direct exchange of produce, sheep, hides, skins, or accidental standards of value, such as shells?

A definite kind of money, whatever it may be, always becomes not a means of exchange, but a means of ransoming from violence; and it begins to circulate among men only when a definite standard is compulsorily required from all.

It is only then that everybody wants it equally, and only then does it receive any value.

And further, it is not the thing that is most convenient for exchange that receives exchange value, but that which is required by the government. If gold is demanded, gold becomes valuable: if knuckle-bones were demanded, they, too, would become valuable. If it were not so, why, then, has the issue of this means of exchange always been the prerogative of the government? The Fiji-Islanders, for instance, have arranged among themselves their own means of exchange; well, then, let them be free to exchange what and how they like, and you, men possessing power, or the means of violence, do not interfere with this exchange. But instead of this you coin money, and do not allow anyone else to coin it; or, as is the case with us, you merely print some notes, engraving upon them the heads of the tsars, sign them with a particular signature, and threaten to punish every falsification of them. Then you distribute this money to your assistants, and, under the name of duties and taxes, you require everybody to give you such money or such notes with such signatures, and so many of them, that a workman must give away all his labour in order to get these notes or coins; and then you want to convince us that this money is necessary for us as a means of exchange!

Here are all men free, and none oppresses the others or keeps them in slavery; but money appears in society and immediately an iron law exists, in consequence of which rent increases and wages diminish to the minimum.

That half (nay, more than half) of the Russian peasants, in order to pay direct and indirect taxes, voluntarily sell themselves as slaves to the land-owners or to manufacturers, does not at all signify (which is obvious); for the violent collection of the poll-taxes and indirect and land taxes, which have to be paid in money to the government and to its assistants (the landowners), *compels* the workman to be a slave to those who own money; but it means that this money, as a means of exchange, and an iron law, exist.

Before the serfs were free, I could compel Iván to do any work; and if he refused to do it, I could send him to the police-sergeant, and the latter would give him the rod till he submitted. But if I compelled Iván to overwork himself, and did not give him either land or food, the matter would go up to the authorities, and I should have to answer for it.

But now that men are free, I can compel Iván and Peter and Sidor to do every kind of work; and if they refuse I give them no money to pay taxes, and then they will be flogged till they submit: besides this, I may also make a German, a Frenchman, a Chinaman, and an Indian, work for me by that means, so that, if they do not submit, I shall not give them money to hire land, or to buy bread, because they have neither land nor bread. And if I make them overwork themselves, or kill them with excess of labour, nobody will say a word to me about it; and, moreover, if I have read books on political economy I shall be quite sure that all men are free and that money does not create slavery!

Our peasants have long known that with a ruble one can hurt more than with a stick. It is only political economists who cannot see it.

To say that money does not create bondage, is the same as to have asserted, fifty years ago, that serfdom did not create slavery. Political economists say that money is an inoffensive medium of exchange, notwithstanding the fact that its possession enables one man to enslave another. Why, then, was it not said half a century ago that servitude was, in itself, an inoffensive medium of reciprocal services, notwithstanding the fact that no man could lawfully enslave another? Some give their manual labour, and the work of others consists in taking care of the physical and intellectual welfare of the slaves, and in superintending their efforts.

And, I fancy, some really did say this.

CHAPTER XIX

If the object of this sham pseudo-science of Political Economy had not been the same as that of all other legal sciences,—the justification of coercion,—it could not have avoided noticing the strange phenomena that the distribution of wealth, the deprivation of some men of land and capital, and the enslavery of some men to others, depend upon money, and that it is only by means of money that some men utilize the labour of others,—in other words, enslave them.

I repeat that a man who has money may buy up and monopolise all the corn and kill others by starvation, completely oppressing them, as it has frequently happened before our own eyes on a very large scale.

It would seem then that we ought to examine the connection of these occurrences with money; but Political Science, with full assurance, asserts that money has no connection whatever with the matter.

This science says, "Money is as much an article of merchandise as anything else which contains the value of its production, only with this difference,—that this article of merchandise is chosen as the more convenient medium of exchange for establishing values, for saving, and for making payments. One man has made boots, another has grown wheat, the third has bred sheep; and now, in order to exchange more conveniently, they put money into circulation, which represents the equivalent of labour; and by this medium they exchange the soles of boots for a loin of mutton, or ten pounds of flour."

Students of this sham science are very fond of picturing to themselves such a state of affairs; but there has never been such a condition in the world. This idea about society is like the fancy about the primitive, prehistoric, perfect human state which the philosophers cherished; but such a state never existed.

In all human societies where money has been used there has also been the oppression by the strong and the armed of the weak and the defenceless; and wherever there was oppression, there the standard of value, money, whatever it consisted of, cattle or hides, skin or metals, must have unavoidably lost its significance as a medium of exchange, and received the meaning of a ransom from violence.

There is no doubt that money does possess the inoffensive properties which science enumerates; but it would have these properties only in a society in which there was no violence,—in an ideal state. But in such a society money would not be found as a general measure of value. In such a community, at the advent of violence, money would immediately lose its significance.

In all societies known to us where money is used it receives the significance of a medium of exchange only because it serves as a means of violence. And its chief object is to act thus,—not as a mere medium. Where violence exists, money cannot be a true medium of exchange, because it is not a measure of value,—because, as soon as one man may take away from another the products of his labour, all measures of value are directly violated. If horses and cows, bred by one man, and violently taken away by others, were brought to a market, it is plain that the value of other horses and cows there, when brought into competition with stolen animals, would no longer correspond with the labour of breeding them. And the value of everything else would also change with this change, and so money could not determine values.

Besides, if one man may acquire by force a cow or a horse or a house, he may by the same force acquire money itself, and with this money acquire all kinds of produce. If, then, money itself is acquired by violence, and spent to purchase products, money entirely loses its quality as a medium of exchange.

The oppressor who takes money and gives it for the products of labour does not exchange anything, but obtains from labour all that he wants.

But let us suppose that such an imaginary and impossible state of society really existed, in which money is in circulation, without the exercise of general violence,—silver or gold serving as a measure of value and as a medium of exchange. All the savings in such a society are expressed by money. There appears in this society an oppressor in the shape of a conqueror. Let us suppose that this oppressor claims the cows, horses, clothes, and the houses of the inhabitants; but, as it is not convenient for him to take possession of all this, he naturally thinks of taking that which represents among these men all kinds of values and is exchanged for everything,—money. And at once in this community, money receives, for the oppressor and his assistants, another signification, and its character as a medium of exchange therefore immediately ceases.

The measure of the values will always depend on the pleasure of the oppressor. The articles most necessary to him, and for which he gives more money, are considered greater value, and *vice versa*; so that, in a community exposed to violence, money at once receives its chief meaning,—it becomes a means of violence and a ransom from violence, and it retains, among the oppressed, its significance as a medium of exchange only so far as that is convenient to the oppressor.

Let us picture the whole affair in a circle, thus:—The serfs supply their landlord with linen, poultry, sheep, and daily labour. The landlord substitutes money for these goods, and fixes the value of the various articles sent in. Those who have no linen, corn, cattle, or manual labour to offer, may bring a definite sum of money.

It is obvious, that, in the society of the peasants of this landlord, the price of the various articles will always depend upon the landlord's pleasure. The landlord uses the articles collected among his peasants, and some of these articles are more necessary for him than others: he fixes the prices for them accordingly, more or less. It is clear that the mere will and requirements of the landlord must regulate the prices of these articles among the payers. If he is in want of corn, he will set a high price for a fixed quantity of it, and a low price for linen, cattle, or work; and therefore those who have no corn will sell their labour, linen, and cattle to others, in order to buy corn to give it to the landlord.

If the landlord chooses to substitute money for all his claims, then the value of things will again depend, not upon the value of labour, but first upon the sum of money which the landlord requires, and secondly upon the articles produced by the peasants, which are more necessary to the landlord, and for which he allows a higher price.

The money-claim made by the landlord on the peasants ceases to influence the prices of the articles only when the peasants of this landlord live separately from other people and have no connection with any one; and secondly, when the landlord employs money, not in purchasing things in his own village, but elsewhere. Only under these two conditions would the prices of things, though changed nominally, remain relatively the same, and money would become a measure of value and a medium of exchange.

But if the peasants have any business connections with the inhabitants surrounding them, the prices of their produce, as sold to their neighbours, would depend on the sum required from them by their landlord. (If less money is required from their neighbours than from themselves, then their products would be sold cheaper than the products of their neighbours, and *vice versa*.) Again, the landlord's money-demand would cease to influence the prices of the articles, only when the sums collected by the landlord were not spent in buying the products of his own peasants. But if he spends the money in purchasing from them, it is plain that the prices of various articles will constantly vary among them according as the landlord buys more of one thing than another.

Suppose one landlord has fixed a very high poll-tax, and his neighbour a very low one: it is clear that on the estate of the first landlord every thing will be cheaper than on the estate of the second, and that the prices on either estate will depend only upon the increase and decrease of the poll-taxes. This is one effect of violence on value.

Another, rising out of the first, consists in relative values. Suppose one landlord is fond of horses, and pays a high price for them; another is fond of towels, and offers a high figure for them. It is obvious that on the estate of either of these two landlords, the horses and the towels will be dear, and the prices of these articles will be out of proportion to those of cows or of corn. If to-morrow the collector of towels dies, and his heirs are fond of poultry, then it is obvious that the price of towels will fall and that of poultry will rise.

Wherever in society there is the mastery of one man over another, there the meaning of money as the measure of value at once yields to the will of the oppressor, and its meaning as a medium of exchange of the products of labour is replaced by another,—that of the most convenient means of utilizing other people's labour.

The oppressor wants money neither as a medium of exchange,—for he takes whatever he wants without exchange,—nor as a measure of value,—for he himself determines the value of everything,—but only for the convenience it affords of exercising violence; and this convenience consists in the fact that money may be stored up, and is the most convenient means of holding in slavery the majority of mankind.

It is not convenient to carry away all the cattle in order always to have horses, cows, and sheep whenever wanted, because they must be fed; the same holds good with corn, for it may be spoiled; the same with slaves; sometimes a man may require thousands of workmen, and sometimes none. Money demanded from those who have not got it makes it possible to get rid of all these inconveniences and to have everything that is required; and this is why the oppressor wants money. Besides which, he wants money so that his right to utilize another man's labour may not be confined to certain men but may be extended to all men who require the money.

When there was no money in circulation each landlord could utilize the labour of his own serfs only; but when they agreed to demand from the peasants money which they had not, they were enabled to appropriate without distinction the labour of all men on every estate.

Thus the oppressor finds it more convenient to press all his claims on labour in the shape of money, and for this sole object is it desired. To the victim from whom it is taken away money cannot be of use, either for the purpose of exchange (seeing he exchanges without money, as all nations have exchanged who had no government); nor for a measure of value, because this is fixed without him; nor for the purpose of saving, because the man whose productions are taken away cannot save; neither for payments, because an oppressed man always has more to pay than to receive; and if he does receive anything, the payment is made, not in money, but in articles of merchandise in either case; whether the workman takes his goods from his master's shop to remunerate his labour, or whether he buys the necessaries of life with his earnings in other shops, the money is required from him, and he is told by his oppressors that if he does not pay it they will refuse to give him land or bread, or will take away his cow or his horse, or condemn him to work, or put him in prison. He can only free himself from all this by selling the products of his toil, his own labour, or that of his children.

He will have to sell this according to the prices established, not by a regular exchange, but by the authority which demands money of him.

Under the conditions of the influence of tribute and taxes on prices,—which everywhere and always repeat themselves, as much with the land-owners in a narrow circle, as with the state on a larger scale (in which the causes of the modification of prices are as obvious to us, as the motion of the hands and feet of puppets is obvious to those who look behind the curtain and see who are the wire-pullers):—under these circumstances, to say that money is a medium of exchange and a measure of value, is at least astonishing.

CHAPTER XX

All slavery is based solely on the fact that one man can deprive another of his life, and by threatening to do so can compel him to do his will. We may see for certain that whenever one man is enslaved by another, when, against his own will and by the will of another, he does certain actions contrary to his inclination, the cause, if traced to its source, is nothing more nor less than a result of this threat. If a man gives to others all his labour, has not enough to eat, has to send his little children from home to work hard, leaves the land, and devotes all his life to a hated and unnecessary task, which happens before our own eyes in the world (which we term civilized because we ourselves live in it), then we may certainly say that he does so only because not to do so would be equivalent to loss of life.

Therefore in our civilized world, where the majority of the people, amidst terrible privations, perform hated labours unnecessary to themselves, the greater number of men are in a slavery based on the threat of being deprived of their existence. Of what, then, does this slavery consist? Wherein lies this power of threat?

In olden times the means of subjugation and the threat to kill were plain and obvious to all: the primitive means of enslaving men then consisted in a direct threat to kill with the sword.

An armed man said to an unarmed, "I can kill thee, as thou hast seen I have done to thy brother, but I do not want to do it: I will spare thee,—first, because it is not agreeable for me to kill thee; secondly, because, as well for me as for thee, it will be more convenient that thou shouldst labour for me than that I should kill thee. Therefore do all I order thee to do, but know that, if thou refusest, I will take thy life."

So the unarmed man submitted to the armed one and did everything he was ordered to do. The unarmed man laboured, the armed threatened. This was that personal slavery which appeared first among all nations, and which still exists among primitive races.

This means of enslaving always begins the work; but when life becomes more complicated it undergoes a change. With the complication of life such a method presents great inconveniences to the oppressor. Before he can appropriate the labour of the weaker he must feed and clothe them and keep them at work, and so their number remains small; and, besides, this compels the slave-holder to remain continually with the slaves, driving them to work by the threat of murdering them. And thus another means of subjugation is developed.

Five thousand years ago (according to the Bible) this novel, convenient, and clever means of oppression was discovered by Joseph the Beautiful.

It is similar to that employed now in the menageries for taming restive horses and wild beasts.

It is hunger!

This contrivance is thus described in the Bible (Genesis xli., 48–57):—

And he (Joseph) gathered up all the food of the seven years, which were in the land of Egypt, and laid up the food in the cities: the food of the field, which was round about every city, laid he up in the same.

And Joseph gathered corn as the sand of the sea, very much, until he left numbering; for it was without number.

And the seven years of plenteousness, that was in the land of Egypt, were ended.

And the seven years of dearth began to come, according as Joseph had said: and the dearth was in all lands; but in all the land of Egypt, there was bread.

And when all the land of Egypt was famished, the people cried to Pharaoh for bread: and Pharaoh said unto all the Egyptians, Go unto Joseph; what he said to you, do.

And the famine was over all the face of the earth: And Joseph opened all the storehouses, and sold unto the Egyptians; and the famine waxed sore in the land of Egypt.

And all countries came into Egypt to Joseph for to buy corn; even because that the famine was so sore in all lands.

Joseph, making use of the primitive means of enslaving men by the threat of the sword, gathered corn during the years of plenty in expectation of years of famine which generally follow years of plenty,—men know all this without the dreams of Pharaoh,—and then by the pangs of hunger he made all the Egyptians and the inhabitants of the surrounding countries slaves to Pharaoh more securely and conveniently. And when the people began to be famished, he arranged matters so as to keep them in his power *forever*.

(Genesis xlvii., 13–26.) And there was no bread in all the land; for the famine was very sore, so that the land of Egypt and all the land of Canaan fainted by reason of the famine.

And Joseph gathered up all the money that was found in the land of Egypt, and in the land of Canaan, for the corn which they bought: and Joseph brought the money into Pharaoh's house.

And when money failed in the land of Egypt, and in the land of Canaan, all the Egyptians came unto Joseph, and said, Give us bread: for why should we die in thy presence? for the money faileth. And Joseph said, Give your cattle; and I will give you for your cattle, if money fail. And they brought their cattle unto Joseph: and Joseph gave them bread in exchange for horses, and for the flocks, and for the cattle of the herds, and for the asses: and he fed them with bread for all their cattle for that year.

When that year was ended, they came unto him the second year, and said unto him, We will not hide it from my Lord, how that our money is spent; my lord also hath our herds of cattle; there is not ought left in the sight of my lord, but our bodies, and our lands: Wherefore shall we die before thine eyes, both we and our land? buy us and our land for bread, and we and our land will be servants unto Pharaoh: and give us seed, that we may live, and not die, and that the land be not desolate. And Joseph bought all the land of Egypt for Pharaoh; for the Egyptians sold every man his field, because the famine prevailed over them: so the land became Pharaoh's. And as for the people, he removed them to cities from one end of the borders of Egypt even to the other end thereof.

Only the lands of the priests bought he not; for the priests had a portion assigned them of Pharaoh, and did eat their portion which Pharaoh gave them: wherefore they sold not their lands.

Then Joseph said unto the people, Behold, I have bought you this day and your land for Pharaoh: lo, here is seed for you, and ye shall sow the land. And it shall come to pass in the increase, that ye shall give the fifth part unto Pharaoh, and four parts shall be your own, for seed of the field, and for your food, and for them of your households, and for food for your little ones.

And they said, Thou hast saved our lives: let us find grace in the sight of my lord, and we will be Pharaoh's servants.

And Joseph made it a law over the land of Egypt unto this day, that Pharaoh should have the fifth part; except the land of the priests only, which became not Pharaoh's.

Formerly, in order to appropriate labour, Pharaoh had to use violence towards them; but now, when the stores and the land belonged to Pharaoh, he had only to keep these stores by force, and hunger compelled the men to labour for him.

All the land now belonged to Pharaoh, and he had all the stores (which were taken away from the people); and therefore, instead of driving them to work individually by the sword, he had only to keep food from them and they were enslaved, not by the sword, but by hunger.

In a year of scarcity, all men may be starved to death at Pharaoh's will; and in a year of plenty, all may be killed who, from casual misfortunes, have no stores of corn.

Thus comes into operation the second means of enslaving, not directly with the sword,—that is, by the strong man driving the weak one to labour under threat of killing him,—but by the strong one having taken away from the weak the stores of corn which, keeping by the sword, he compels the weak to work for.

Joseph said to the hungry men, "I could starve you to death, because I have the corn; but I will spare your lives, but only under the condition that you do all I order you for the food which I will give you." For the first means of enslaving, the oppressor only needs soldiers to ride to and fro among the inhabitants, and make them fulfil the requirements of their master under threat of death. And thus the oppressor has only to pay his soldiers. But with the second means, besides the soldiers, the oppressor must have different assistants for keeping and protecting the land and stores from the starving people.

These are the Josephs and their stewards and distributors. And the oppressor has to reward them, and to give Joseph a dress of brocade, a gold ring, and servants, and corn and silver to his brothers and relatives. Besides this, from the very nature of the second means, not only the stewards and their relations, but all who have stores of corn become participators in this violence, just as by the first means, based upon immediate force, every one who has arms becomes a partner in tyranny, so by this means, based upon hunger, every one who has stores of provision shares in it, and has power over those who have no stores.

The advantage of this method over the former consists, first and chiefly, in the fact that the oppressor need no longer compel the workmen to do his will by force, for they themselves come to him and sell themselves to him; secondly, in the circumstance that fewer men escape from his violence. The drawback is, that he has to employ a greater number of men. For the oppressed the advantage of it consists in the fact that they are no longer exposed to rough violence but are left to themselves; and can always hope to pass from being the oppressed to becoming oppressors in their turn, which by fortunate circumstances they sometimes really do. The drawback for them is, that they can never escape from participating in the oppression of others.

This new means of enslaving generally comes into operation together with the old one; and the oppressor lessens the one and increases the other according to his desires. But this does not fully satisfy the man who wishes to take away as much as possible of the products of the labour of as many working-people as he can find, and to enslave as many men as possible; and, therefore, a third means of oppression is evolved.

This is the slavery of taxation, and, like the second, it is based upon hunger; but to the means of subduing men by depriving them of bread is added the deprivation of other necessaries.

The oppressor requires from the slaves so much of the money he himself has coined, that, in order to obtain it, the slaves are compelled to sell not only stores of corn in greater quantity than the fifth part which was fixed by Joseph, but the first necessaries of life as well,—meat, skins, wool, clothes, firewood, even their buildings; and therefore the oppressor always keeps his slaves in his power, not only by hunger, but by thirst, cold and other privations.

And thus the third means of slavery comes into operation, a monetary, tributary one, consisting in the oppressor saying to the oppressed, "I can do with each of you just what I like; I can kill and destroy you by taking away the land by which you earn your living; I can, with this money which you must give me, buy all the corn upon which you feed, and sell it to strangers, and at any time annihilate you by starvation; I can take from you all that you have,—your cattle, your houses, your clothes; but it is neither convenient nor agreeable for me to do so, and therefore I let you alone, to work as you please; only give me so much of the money which I demand of you, either as a poll-tax, or according to your land or the quantity of your food and drink, or your clothes or your houses. Give me this money, and do what you like among yourselves, but know that I shall neither protect nor maintain widows nor orphans nor invalids nor old people, nor such as have been burned out: I shall only protect the regular circulation of this money. This right will always be mine, to protect only those who regularly give me the fixed number of these pieces of money: as to how or where you get it, I shall not in the least trouble myself." And so the oppressor distributes these pieces of money as an acknowledgement that his demand has been complied with.

The second method of enslaving consisted in this, that, having taken away the fifth part of the harvest, and collected stores of corn, Pharaoh, besides the personal slavery by the sword, received, by his assistants, the possibility of dominion over the working-people during the time of famine, and over some of them during misfortunes which happen to them.

The third method consists in this: Pharaoh requires from the working-people more money than the value of the fifth part of corn which he took from them; he and his assistants get a new means of dominion over the working-class, not merely during the famine and their casual misfortunes, but permanently.

By the second method, men retain some stores of corn which help them to bear indifferent harvests and casual misfortunes without going into slavery; but by the third, when there are more demands, the stores, not of corn only but of all other necessaries of life are taken away from them, and at the first misfortune a workman, having neither stores of corn nor any other stores which he might exchange for corn, falls into slavery to those who have money.

To set the first in motion an oppressor need have only soldiers, and share the booty with them; for the second, besides the protectors of the land and the stores, he must have collectors and clerks for the distribution of the corn; for the third, besides the soldiers for keeping the land and his property, he must have collectors of taxes, assessors of direct taxation, supervisors, custom-house clerks, managers of money, and coiners of it.

The organization of the third method is much more complicated than that of the second. By the second, the getting in of corn may be leased out, as was done in olden times and is still the custom in Turkey; but by putting taxes on men there is need of a complicated administration, which has to ensure the right levying of the taxes. And therefore by the third method the oppressor has to share the plunder with a still greater number of men than by the second; besides, according to the very nature of the thing, all the men of the same or of the foreign country who possess money become sharers with the oppressed.

The advantage of the third method over the first and second consists chiefly in the following fact: that by it there is no need to wait for a year of scarcity, as in the time of Joseph, but years of famine are established forever, and (whilst by the second method the part of the labour which is taken away depends upon the harvest, and cannot be augmented *ad libitum*, because if there is no corn, there is nothing to take) by the new *monetary* method the requirement can be brought to any desired limit, for the demand for money can always be satisfied, because the debtor, to satisfy it, must sell his cattle, clothes, or houses. The chief advantage to the oppressor of this method is that he can take away the greatest quantity of labour in the most convenient way; for a money-tax, like a screw, may easily and conveniently be turned to the utmost limit, and golden eggs be obtained though the bird that lays them is all but dead.

Another of its advantages for the oppressor is that its violence reaches all those also who, by possessing no land, formerly escaped from it by giving only a part of their labour for corn; whereas now, besides that part which they give for corn, they must now give another part for taxes. A drawback for the oppressor is that he has to share the plunder with a still greater number of men, not only with his direct assistants, but also with all those men of his own country, and even of foreign countries, who may have the money which is demanded from the slaves.

Its advantage for the oppressed is only that he is allowed greater independence than under the second method; he may live where he chooses, do what he likes; he may sow or not sow; he has to give no account of his labour; and if he has money, he may consider himself entirely free, and constantly hope, though only for a time, to obtain not only an independent position, but even to become an oppressor himself, when he has money to spare.

The drawback for the oppressed is, that on a general average their situation becomes much worse, and they are deprived of the greater part of the products of their labour, because the number of those who utilize their labour has increased, and therefore the burden of keeping them falls upon a smaller number of men.

This third method of enslaving men is also very old, and comes into operation with the former two without entirely excluding them.

These three methods of enslaving men have always been in operation.

They may all be compared to screws which secure the board laid on the work-people which presses them down. The fundamental, or middle screw, without which the other screws could not hold, which is first screwed up, and which is never slackened, is the screw of personal slavery, the enslaving of some men by others under threat of slaughter; the second, which is screwed up after the first, is that of enslaving men by taking away the land and stores of provisions from them, such alienation being maintained by the threat to murder; and the third screw is slavery enforced by the requirement of certain money taxes; and this demand is also maintained under threat of murder.

These three screws are made fast, and it is only when one of them is tightened more that the others are slackened. For the complete enslavement of the workman, all three are necessary; and in our society, all three are in operation together. The first method of personal slavery under threat of murder by the sword has never been abolished, and never will be so long as there is any oppression, because every kind of oppression is based on this alone.

We are all quite sure that personal slavery is abolished in our civilized world; that the last remnant of it has been annihilated in America and in Russia, and that it is only among the barbarians that real slavery exists, and that with us it is no longer in being. We forget only one small circumstance,—those hundreds of millions of standing troops without which no state exists, and with the abolition of which all the economical organization of each state would inevitably fall to pieces. Yet what are these millions of soldiers but the personal slaves of those who rule them? Are not these men compelled to do the will of their commanders under the threat of torture and death,—a threat often carried out? the difference consisting only in the fact that the submission of these slaves is not called slavery, but discipline, and that slaves are slaves from their birth, but soldiers only during a more or less short period of their so-called "service."

Personal slavery, therefore, is not only not abolished in our civilized world, but, under the system of conscription, it has of late years been confirmed; and it has remained as it has always existed, only slightly changed from its original form. And it cannot but exist, because, so long as there is the enslaving of one man by another there will be this personal slavery too, this slavery which, under the threat of the sword, maintains serfdom, land-ownership, and taxes.

It may be that this slavery of troops is useful, as it is said, for the defence and the glory of the country; but this kind of utility is more than doubtful, because we see how often in the case of unsuccessful wars it serves only for the subjugation and shame of the country. But of the expediency of this slavery for maintaining that of the land and taxes there is no question.

If Irish or Russian peasants were to take possession of the land of the proprietors, troops would be sent to dispossess them. If you build a distillery or a brewery and do not pay excise, then soldiers will be sent to shut it up. Refuse to pay taxes, and the same thing will happen to you.

The second screw is the method of enslaving men by taking away from them their land and their stores of provisions. This method has also always been in existence wherever men are oppressed; and, whatever changes it may undergo, it is everywhere in operation.

Sometimes all the land belongs to the sovereign, as in Turkey, and there one-tenth is given to the state treasury. Sometimes a part of the land belongs to the sovereign, and taxes are raised on it. Sometimes all the land belongs to a few people and is let out for labour, as in England. Sometimes more or less large portions of land belong to the land-owners, as in Russia, Germany, and France. But wherever there is enslaving there exists also the appropriation of the land by the oppressor, and this screw is slackened or tightened only according to the condition of the other screws.

Thus, in Russia, when personal slavery was extended to the majority of the working-people there was no need of land-slavery; but the screw of personal slavery was slackened in Russia only when the screws of land and tax slavery were tightened. Only when the government had appropriated the land and divided it among private individuals, and had instituted money payments and taxation, did it give the peasants personal freedom.

In England, for instance, land-slavery is pre-eminently in operation, and the question about the nationalizing of the land consists only in the screw of taxation being tightened in order that the screw of land appropriation may be slackened.

The third method of enslaving men, by taxes, has also been in operation for ages; and in our days, with the extension of uniform standards of money and the strengthening of state powers it has become an especially powerful influence.

This method is so developed in our days that it tends to be a substitute for the second method of enslaving,—the land monopoly.

It is obvious from the state of the political economy of all Europe, that it is by the tightening of this screw that the screw of land slavery is slackened.

In our own lifetime we have witnessed in Russia two transformations of slavery. When the serfs were liberated, and their landlords retained the right to the greater part of the soil, the landlords were afraid they would lose their power; but experience has shown that having let go the whole chain of personal slavery, they had only to seize another,—that of the land. A peasant was short of corn; he had not enough to live on. The landlord had land and stores of corn: and therefore the peasant still remained the same slave.

Another transformation was caused by the government screw of taxation being pressed home. The majority of working-people, having no stores, were obliged to sell themselves to their landlords and to the factories. This new form of oppression held the people still tighter, so that nine-tenths of the Russian working-people are still working for their landlords and in the factories to pay these taxes. This is so obvious, that, if the government were to remit taxation for one year only, all labour would be stopped in the fields of the landlords, and in the factories. Nine-tenths of the Russian people hire themselves out during and before the collection of taxes.

All these three methods have never ceased to operate, and are still in operation, but people are inclined to ignore them or to invent new excuses for them. And, what is most remarkable of all is, that the very means on which everything is based, that screw which is screwed up tighter than all others, which holds everything at the moment in question, is not noticed so long as it holds. When in the ancient world the entire economical order was upheld by personal slavery, the greatest intellects did not notice it. To Plato, as well as to Xenophon, and Aristotle, and to the Romans, it seemed that it could not be otherwise, and that slavery was an unavoidable and natural result of wars, without which the existence of mankind was inconceivable. Similarly, in the Middle Ages, and till recently, people did not apprehend the meaning of land-ownership, on which depended the entire economical organization of their time.

So also, at present, no one sees or wants to see, that in our time the slavery of the majority of the people depends on taxes collected by the government from its own land slaves, taxes collected *by administration and the troops,*—by the very same troops which are maintained by these taxes.

CHAPTER XXI

No wonder that the slaves themselves, who have always been enslaved, do not understand their own position, and that this condition in which they have always lived is considered by them to be natural to human life, and that they hail as a relief any change in their form of slavery; no wonder that their owners sometimes quite sincerely think they are, in a measure, freeing the slaves by slacking one screw, though they are compelled to do so by the over-tension of another.

Both become accustomed to their state; and the slaves, never having known what freedom is, merely seek an alleviation, or only the change of their condition; the other, the owners, wishing to mask their injustice, try to assign a particular meaning to those new forms of slavery which they enforce in place of the older ones. But it is wonderful how the majority of the critics of the economic conditions of the life of the people fail to see that which forms the basis of the entire economic conditions of a people.

One would think the duty of a true science would be to try to ascertain the connection of the phenomena and general cause of a series of occurrences. But the majority of the representatives of modern Political Economy are doing just the reverse of this: they carefully hide the connection and meaning of the phenomena, and avoid answering the most simple and essential questions.

Modern Political Economy, like an idle, lazy cart-horse, goes well only down-hill, when it has no collar-work; but as soon as it has anything to draw, it at once refuses, pretending it has to go somewhere aside after its own business. When any grave, essential question is put to Political Economy, scientific discussions are started about some other matter having only in view to divert attention from this subject.

You ask, "How are we to account for a fact so unnatural, monstrous, unreasonable, and not useless only, but harmful, that some men can eat or work only according to the will of other men?"

You are gravely answered, "Because some men must arrange the labour and feeding of others, such is the law of production."

You ask, "What is this property-right which allows some men to appropriate to themselves the land, food, and instruments of labour belonging to others?" You are again gravely answered, "This right is based upon the protection of labour,"—that is, the protection of some men's labour is effected by taking possession of the labour of other men.

You ask, "What is that money which is everywhere coined and stamped by the governments, by the authorities, and which is so exorbitantly demanded from the working-people, and which in the shape of national debts is levied upon the future generations of workingmen? Further, has not this money, demanded from the people in the shape of taxes which are raised to the utmost pitch, has not this money any influence on the economic relationships of men,—between the payers and the receivers?" And you are answered in all seriousness, "Money is an article of merchandise like sugar, or chintz; and it differs from other articles only in the fact that it is more convenient for exchange."

As for the influence of taxes on the economic conditions of a people, it is a different question altogether: the laws of production, exchange, and distribution of wealth, are one thing, but taxation is quite another. You ask whether it has any influence on the economic conditions of a people that the government can arbitrarily raise or lower prices, and, having increased the taxes, can make slaves of all who have no land? The pompous answer is, "The laws of production, exchange, and distribution of wealth constitute one science,—Political Economy; and taxes, and, generally speaking, State Economy, come under another head,—the Law of Finance."

You ask finally, "Is no influence exercised on economic conditions by the circumstance that all the people are in bondage to the government, and that this government can arbitrarily ruin them all, can take away all the products of their labour, and even carry the men themselves away from their work into military slavery?" You are answered, "This is altogether a different question, belonging to the State Law."

The majority of the representatives of science discuss quite seriously the laws of the economic life of a people, while all the functions and activities of this life are dependent on the will of the oppressor. Whilst they recognize the influence of the oppressor as a natural condition of a nation's life, they do just what a critic of the economic conditions of the life of the personal slaves of different masters would do, were he to omit to consider the influence exercised on the life of these slaves by the will of that master who compels them to work on this or that thing and drives them from one place to another according to his pleasure, who feeds them or neglects to do so, who kills them or leaves them alive.

A noxious superstition has been long in existence and still survives,—a superstition which has done more harm to men than the most terrible religious superstitions.

And so-called science supports this superstition with all its power, and with the utmost zeal. This superstition exactly resembles religious superstitions. It consists in affirming that, besides the duties of man to man, there are still more important duties towards an imaginary being,—which the theologians call God, and the political scientists the State.

The religious superstition consists in affirming that sacrifices, even of human lives, must be offered to this imaginary being, and that they can and ought to be enforced by every means, even by violence. The political superstition consists in the belief that, besides the duties of man to man, there are still more important duties to an imaginary being, the State; and the offerings,—often of human lives,—brought to this imaginary being are also essential, and can and ought to be enforced by every means, even by violence.

This superstition it is, formerly encouraged by the priests of different religions, which is now sustained by so-called science.

Men are thrown into slavery, into the most terrible slavery, worse than has ever before existed; but Political Science tries to persuade men that it is necessary and unavoidable.

The state must exist for the welfare of the people, and it must do its duty, to rule and protect them from their enemies. For this purpose the state needs money and troops. Money must be subscribed by all the citizens of the state. And hence all the relations of men must be considered in the light of the existence of the state.

"I want to help my father by my labour," says a common unlearned man. "I want also to marry; but instead, I am taken and sent to Kazan, to be a soldier for six years. I leave the military service, I want to plough the ground to earn food and drink for my family; but I am not allowed to plough for a hundred versts around me unless I pay money, which I have not got, and pay it to those men who do not know how to plough, and who demand for the land so much money that I must give them all my labour to procure it: however, I still manage to save something, and wish to give this to my children; but a police official comes and takes from me all I had saved, for taxes: I can earn a little more, and again I am deprived of it. My entire economic activity is at the mercy of state demands; and it seems to me that my position and that of my brethren, will certainly improve if we are liberated from the demands of the state."

But he is told, "Such reasoning is the result of your ignorance. Study the laws of production, exchange, and distribution of wealth, and do not mix up economical questions with those of the state. The phenomena which you point to are no restraints on your freedom; they are the necessary sacrifices which you, along with others, must make for your own freedom and welfare."

"But my son has been taken away from me," says again a common man; "and they threaten to take away all my sons as soon as they are grown up: they took him away by force, and drove him to face the enemy's guns in some country which we have never heard of, and for an object which we cannot understand.

"And as for the land which they will not allow us to plough, and for want of which we are starving, it belongs to a man who got possession of it by force, and whom we have never seen, and whose usefulness we cannot even understand. And the taxes, to collect which the police official has by force taken my cow from my children, will, so far as I know, go to this same man who took my cow away, and to various members of the committees and of departments which I do not know of, and in the utility of which I do not believe. How is it, then, that all these acts of violence secure my liberty, and all this evil procures good?"

You may compel a man to be a slave and to do that which he considers to be evil for himself, but you cannot compel him to think, that, in suffering violence, he is free, and that the obvious evil which he endures constitutes his good. This appears impossible. Yet by the help of science this very thing has been done in our time.

The state, that is, the armed oppressors, decide what they want from those whom they oppress (as in the case of England and the Fiji-Islanders): they decide how much labour they want from their slaves,—they decide how many assistants they will need in collecting the fruits of this labour; they organize their assistants in the shape of soldiers, land-owners, and collectors of taxes. And the slaves give their labour, and, at the same time, believe that they give it, not because their masters demand it, but for the sake of their own freedom and welfare; and that this service and these bloody sacrifices to the divinity called the State are necessary, and that, except this service to their Deity, they are free. They believe this because the same had been formerly said in the name of religion by the priests, and is now said in the name of so-called science, by learned men.

But one need only cease to believe what is said by these other men who call themselves priests or learned men, for the absurdity of such an assertion to become obvious.

The men who oppress others assure them that this oppression is necessary for the state,—and the state is necessary for the freedom and welfare of men; so that it appears that the oppressors oppress men for the sake of their freedom, and do them evil for the sake of good.

But men are furnished with reason so that they may understand wherein consists their own good, and do it willingly.

As for the acts, the goodness of which is not intelligible to men, and to which they are compelled by force, these cannot be for their good, because a reasoning being can consider as good only the thing which appears so to his reason. If men are driven to evil through passion or folly, all that those who are not so driven can do is to persuade the others into what constitutes their real good. You may try to persuade men that their welfare will be greater when they are all soldiers, are deprived of land, and have given their entire labour away for taxes; but until all men consider this condition to be welfare, and undertake it willingly, one cannot call such a state of things the common welfare of men.

The sole criterion of a good conception is its willing acceptance by men. And the lives of men abound with such acts. Ten workmen buy tools in common, in order to work together with them, and in so doing they are undoubtedly benefitting themselves; but we cannot suppose that if these ten workmen were to compel an eleventh, by force, to join in their association, they would insist that their common welfare will be the same for him.

So with gentlemen who agree to give a subscription dinner at a pound a head to a mutual friend; no one can assert that such a dinner will benefit a man who, against his will, has been obliged to pay a sovereign for it. And so with peasants who decide, for their common convenience, to dig a pond. To those who consider the existence of a pond more valuable than the labour spent on it, digging it will be a common good. But to the one who considers the pond of less value than a day's harvesting in which he is behind-hand, digging it will appear evil. The same holds good with roads, churches, and museums, and with all various social and state affairs.

All such work may be good for those who consider it good, and who therefore freely and willingly perform it,—the dinner which the gentlemen give, the pond which the peasants dig. But work to which men must be driven by force ceases to be a common good precisely by the fact of such violence.

All this is so plain and simple, that, if men had not been so long deceived, there would be no need to explain it.

Suppose we live in a village where all the inhabitants have agreed to build a road over a swamp which is a danger to them. We agree together, and each house promises to give so much money or wood or days of labour. We agree to this because the making of the road is more advantageous to us than what we exchange for it; but among us there are some for whom it is more advantageous to do without a road than to spend money on it, or who at all events think so. Can compelling these men to labour make it of advantage to them? Obviously not; because those who considered that their choosing to join in making the way would have been disadvantageous, will consider it *a fortiori* still more disadvantageous when they are *compelled* to do so. Suppose, even, that we all, without exception, were agreed, and promised so much money or labour from each house, but that it happened that some of those who had promised did not give what they agreed, their circumstances having meanwhile changed, so that it was more advantageous for such now to be without the road than to spend money on it; or that they have simply changed their mind about it; or even calculate that others will make the road without them and that they will then use it. Can coercing these men to join in the labour make them consider that the sacrifices are enforced for their own good?

Obviously not; because, if these men have not fulfilled what they promised, owing to a change in circumstances, so that now the sacrifices for the sake of the road outbalance their gain by it, the compulsory sacrifices of such would be only a worse evil. But if those who refuse to join in building the road intend to utilize the labour of the others, then in this case also coercing them into making a sacrifice would be only a punishment on a supposition, and their object, which nobody can prove, will be punished before it is made apparent; but in neither case can coercing them to join in a work which they do not desire be good for them.

If this is so with sacrifices for a work which every one can comprehend, obvious, and undoubtedly useful to everyone, such as a road over a swamp; how still more unjust and unreasonable is it to coerce millions of men into making sacrifices for objects which are incomprehensible, imperceptible, and often undoubtedly harmful, such as military service and taxation.

But, according to science, what appears to every one to be an evil is a common good: it appears that there are men, a small minority, who alone know of what the common good consists, and, notwithstanding the fact that all other men consider this good to be an evil, this minority can compel the others to do whatever they may consider to be for the common good. And it is this belief which constitutes the chief superstition and the chief deceit and hinders the progress of mankind towards the True and the Good.

To nurse this superstitious deceit has been the object of political sciences in general, and of so-called "Political Economy" in particular.

Many are making use of its aims in order to hide from men the state of oppression and slavery in which they now are.

The way they set about doing so is by starting the theory that the violence connected with the economy of social slavery is a natural and unavoidable evil; and men thereby are deceived and turn their eyes from the real causes of their misfortunes.

Slavery has long been abolished. It has been abolished in Rome as well as in America, and in Russia; but only the word has been abolished,—not the evil.

Slavery is the violent freeing of some men from the labour necessary for satisfying their wants, which transfers this labour to others; and wherever there is a man who does not work, not because others willingly and lovingly work for him, but because he has the possibility, while not working himself, to make others work for him, there slavery exists.

Wherever there are, as in all European societies, men who utilize the labour of thousands of others by coercion, and consider such to be their right, and others who submit to this coercion considering it to be their duty,—there you have slavery in its most dreadful proportions.

Slavery exists. In what, then, does it consist? Slavery consists of that of which it has always consisted, and without which it cannot exist at all,—in the coercion of a weak and unarmed man by a strong and armed man.

Slavery in its three fundamental modes of operation,—personal violence, the military, land-taxes,—maintained by the military, and direct and indirect taxes put upon all the inhabitants, is still in operation now as it has been before.

We do not see it because each of these three forms of slavery has received a new justification, which hides its meaning from us.

The personal violence of armed over unarmed men has been justified as the defence of one's country from imaginary enemies,—while in its essence it has the one old meaning, the submission of the conquered to the oppressors.

The violent seizure of the labourers' land has been justified as the recompense for services rendered to an imaginary common welfare, and confirmed by the right of heritage; but in reality it is the same dispossession of men from their land and enslaving them which was performed by the troops.

And the last, the monetary violence by means of taxes, the strongest and most effective in our days, has received a most wonderful justification.

Dispossessing men of their liberty and their goods is said to be done for the sake of the common liberty and of the common welfare. But in fact it is the same slavery, only an impersonal one.

Wherever violence becomes law, there is slavery.

Whether violence finds its expression in the circumstance that princes with their courtiers come, kill, and burn down villages; whether slave-owners take labour or money for the land from their slaves, and enforce payment by means of armed men, or by putting taxes on others, and riding armed to and fro in the villages; or whether a Home Department collects money through governors or police sergeants,—in one word, as long as violence is maintained by the bayonet,—there will be no distribution of wealth, but it will be accumulated among the oppressors.

As a striking illustration of the truth of this assertion the project of Henry George to nationalize the land may serve us. Henry George proposes to declare all land the property of the state, and to substitute a land-rent for all taxes, direct and indirect. That is, everyone who utilizes the land would have to pay to the state the value of its rent.

What would be the result? The land would belong to the state,—English land to England, American land to America, and so on; that is, there would be slavery, determined by the quantity of cultivated land. It might be that the condition of some labourers would improve; but while a forcible demand for rent remained, the slavery would remain too. The cultivator, after a bad harvest, being unable to pay the rent exacted of him by force, would be obliged to enslave himself to any one who happened to have the money in order not to lose everything and to retain the land.

If a pail leaks, there must be a hole. Looking at the pail, we might imagine the water runs from many holes; but no matter how we might try to stop the imaginary holes from without, the water would not cease running. In order to put a stop to the leakage we must find the place from which water runs, and stop it from the inside.

The same holds good with the proposed means of stopping the irregular distribution of wealth,—the holes through which the wealth runs away from the people.

It is said, *Organize workmen's corporations, make capital social property, make land social property*. All this is only mere stopping from the outside those holes from which we fancy the water runs. In order to stop the wealth going from the hands of the workers to those of the non-workers, it is necessary to try to find from the inside the hole through which this leakage takes place. And this hole is the violence of armed men towards unarmed men, the violence of troops, by means of which men are carried away from their labour, and the land, and the products of labour, taken from them.

So long as there is one armed man, whoever he may be, with the acknowledged right to kill another man, so long will there also exist an unjust distribution of wealth,—in other words, slavery.

I was led into the error that I can help others by the fact that I imagined my money was as good as Semion's. But it was not so.

The general opinion is that money represents wealth; that wealth is the result of work and therefore that money represents work. This opinion is as just as the opinion asserting that every form of state is the result of a contract (contrat social).

All men like to believe that money is only a means of exchange of labour. I have made boots, you have made bread, he has fed sheep; now, in order to exchange our wares the more conveniently, we introduce money, which represents the corresponding share of labour, and through it we exchange leather soles for a mutton brisket and ten pounds of flour.

By means of money we exchange our products and this money, belonging to each of us, represents our labour. This is perfectly true, but true only while in the community, where this exchange takes place, violence of one man towards another did not appear, violence not only over another man's labour, as happens in war and in slavery, but not even violence applied to defend the products of labour of one man against another. This could be only in a community whose members entirely fulfil the Christian law,—in a community where one gets what he demands and where one is not requested to return what he gets. But as soon as violence in any form is applied in the community, the meaning of money for its owner at once loses its significance as a representative of labour, and acquires the significance of a right, based not on labour, but on violence.

As soon as there is war and one man has taken away something from another, then money cannot always represent labour; the money received by the soldier for the booty he has sold, as well as the money got by his superior, is by no means the produce of their work and has quite a different meaning from the money received for the labour resulting in boots. When there are slave-owners and slaves, as have been always in the world, then one cannot assert that money represents labour. The women have woven a quantity of linen, have sold it and received money; the serfs have woven some linen for their master, and the master has sold it and received money. The one and the other money are the same; but one is the product of labour and the other is the product of violence. Likewise, if somebody,—say my father,—made me a present of money and he, when giving it to me, knew, and I knew and everybody knew, that no one can take this money away from me, that if anybody tried to take it, or even merely failed to return it at the date promised, then the authorities would defend me and by force compel the man to return me this money,—then again it is evident that by no means can this money be called a representative of labour, like the money which Semion got for cutting wood.

Thus in a community, where by some kind of violence somebody's money is taken possession of, or the ownership of somebody's money defended against others—there money cannot always represent labour. It represents in such a community sometimes labour, sometimes violence.

So it would be if only one fact of violence of one man over another appeared in the midst of perfectly free relations; but now, when the accumulated money has passed through centuries of most various forms of violence, when these acts of violence continue under other forms; when money itself by its accumulation creates violence,—which is recognized by everybody,—when the direct products of labour constitute only a small part of money made up of all sorts of violence,—to assert now that money represents the work of its owner is an obvious error, or an open lie. One may say it ought to be so, one may say it is desirable that it should be so, but by no means can any one say that it is so.

Money represents labour. Yes; money represents labour, but whose labour? In our society it is only in the rarest cases that money represents the work of its owner. Almost always it represents the labour of other men,—the past or future labours of men. It is the representative of a claim on the labour of other men by force of violence.

Money, in its most exact and at the same time its simplest definition, represents conventional signs, which bestow the right,—or rather the possibility,—to use the work of other men. In its ideal meaning, money ought to give this right or possibility only when it serves itself as a representative of labour, and as such, money could exist in a society devoid of any kind of violence. But as soon as violence takes place in a society, i.e., the possibility of the utilizing of the labour of others by the idler,—then this possibility of using the labour of others, without defining persons over which this violence is committed, is also exercised in money.

The landowner taxed his serfs by a contribution in kind, making them bring a certain quantity of linen, corn, cattle, or a corresponding amount of money. One household delivered the cattle, but the linens were replaced by money. The landowner accepts the money in a certain quantity, only because he knows that for this money he can get the same pieces of linen (generally he takes a little more money to be sure that he will receive for it the same quantity of linen), and this money evidently offers for the landowner lien on other men's labour.

The peasant gives money as a security against persons unknown but numerous, who would undertake to work out so much linen for this money. Those who will undertake to work the linen will do it because they did not succeed in feeding the sheep, and for these they must pay in money; and the peasant who will get the money for the sheep will take it, only because he must pay for the corn, which was a failure that year. The same goes on in the State and all over the world.

A man sells the produce of his past, present or future labour, sometimes his food-stuff, not mostly because money is a convenient exchange for him,—he would exchange without money,—but because he is required by means of violence to give money, as a security on his work.

When Pharaoh has demanded the labour of his slaves, then the slaves have given him all their labour, but they could give only the past and present labour, and could not give that of the future. But with the spread of money tokens and their result of "credit" it becomes possible to give also one's future work for money.

Money, with the existence of violence in society, offers the means for a new form of impersonal slavery, which replaces the personal one. A slave-owner claims a right to the work of Peter, Iván, Sidor. But wherever money is required from everybody, the owner of money acquires a claim on the labour of all those unknown people who are in need of money. Money removes the painful side of slavery, by which the owner knows about his right on Iván, at the same time it removes all those human relations between the owner and the slave, which softened down the burden of personal slavery.

I will not dwell on the theory that perhaps such a state is necessary for the development of mankind, for its progress and so forth—I will not dispute it. I only strive to make clear to myself the conception of money and to discover the general misconception I have made in accepting money, as a representative of labour. I became convinced by experience that money is not a representative of labour, but in the great majority of cases is a representative of violence, or of specially complex artifices founded on violence.

Money in our time has already altogether lost the desirable significance of being the representative of labour; such significance it may have in exceptional cases, but as a rule it has become the right or the possibility of using the labour of others.

This spreading of money, of credit and different conventional signs, more and more confirm this meaning of money. Money is the possibility or the right to use the labours of others.

Money is a new form of slavery differing from the old form of slavery only by its impersonality, by the freedom it gives from all human relations to the slave.

Money is money, a value always equal to itself, and which is always considered quite correct and lawful, and the use of which is not considered immoral, as slavery was.

In my young days a game of lotto was introduced in the clubs. All eagerly played the game and, as was said, many lost their fortunes, ruined their families, lost money entrusted to them, and government funds, and finally shot themselves, so that the game was forbidden and is still forbidden.

I remember I have met old, hardened card players who told me that this game was especially fascinating, because one did not know whom one was to beat, as is the case in other games; the attendant does not even serve one with money, but with counters, everybody loses a small stake and does not betray grief. It is the same in roulette, which is rightly forbidden everywhere.

So it is with money. I have a magical, everlasting ruble; I cut off coupons and live apart from all the affairs of the world. Whom do I harm? I am the most quiet and kind-hearted man. But this is only a game of lotto or roulette where I do not see the man, who shoots himself after having lost, and who provides for me these small coupons, which I carefully cut off under the right angle from the tickets.

I have done nothing, I am doing nothing, and never will do anything, save cut off the coupons, and firmly believe that money represents labour. This is really astounding! And people talk of lunatics! But what mania could be more horrible than this? An intelligent, learned, and in all other respects sensible man lives madly, and soothes himself by not acknowledging that one thing which he should acknowledge to make his argument reasonable, and he considers himself in the right! The coupons are representatives of labour! Of labour! Yes, but of whose labour? Not of his, who owns them, evidently, but of the one who works.

Money is the same as slavery; its aim is the same and its consequences are the same. Its aim is the freeing of some men from the original law, truly called so by a thoughtful writer of the working-classes, from the natural law of life, as we call it, from the law of personal labour for the satisfaction of one's needs. The consequences of the slavery for the owner: the begetting, the invention of infinitely more and more needs never to be satisfied, of effeminate wretchedness and of depravity, and for the slaves,— oppression of the man, and his lowering to the level of a beast.

Money is a new and terrible form of slavery and, like the old form of personal slavery, it equally demoralises the slave and the slave-owner, but it is so much worse, because it frees the slave and the slave-owner from personal human relations.

CHAPTER XXII

I always wonder at the often repeated words, "Yes, it is all true in theory, but how is it in practice?" As though the theory were only a collection of words useful for conversation, and not as though all practice,—that is, all activity of life—were inevitably based upon it.

There must have been an immense number of foolish theories in the world for men to employ such wonderful reasoning. We know that theory is what a man thinks about a thing, and practice is what he does. How can a man think that he ought to act in one way, and then do quite the reverse? If the theory of baking bread consists in this, that first of all one must knead the dough, then put it by to rise, anyone knowing it would be a fool to do the reverse. But with us it has come into fashion to say, "It is all very well in theory, but how would it be in practice?"

In all that has occupied me practice has unavoidably followed theory, not mainly in order to justify it, but because it could not help doing so: if I have understood the affair upon which I have meditated I cannot help doing it in the way in which I have understood it.

I wished to help the needy only because I had money to spare: and I shared the general superstition that money represents labour, and, generally speaking, is something lawful and good in itself. But, having begun to give this money away, I saw that I was only drawing bills of exchange collected from poor people; that I was doing the very thing the old landlords used to do in compelling some of their serfs to work for other serfs.

I saw that every use of money, whether buying anything with it, or giving it away gratis, is a drawing of bills of exchange on poor people, or passing them to others to be drawn by them. And therefore I clearly understood the foolishness of what I was doing in helping the poor by exacting money from them.

I saw that money in itself was not only not a good thing, but obviously an evil one, depriving men of their chief good, labour, and that this very good I cannot give to anyone because I am myself deprived of it: I have neither labour nor the happiness of utilizing my labour.

It might be asked by some, "What is there so peculiarly important in abstractly discussing the meaning of money?" But this argument which I have opened is not merely for the sake of discussion, but in order to find an answer to the vital question which had caused me so much suffering, and on which my life depended, in order to discover what I was to do.

As soon as I understood what wealth means, what money means, then it became clear and certain what I have to do, it became clear and certain what all others have to do,—and that they will inevitably do it, what all men must do. In reality I merely came to realize what I have long known,—that truth which has been transmitted to men from the oldest times, by Buddha, by Isaiah, by Laotse, by Socrates, and most clearly and definitely by Jesus and his predecessor John the Baptist.

John the Baptist, in answer to men's question "What shall we do then?" answered plainly and briefly, "He that hath two coats, let him impart to him that hath none; and he that hath meat, let him do likewise" (Luke iii., 10, 11).

The same thing, and with still greater clearness, said Jesus,—blessing the poor, and uttering woes on the rich. He said that no man can serve God and mammon. He forbade his disciples not only to take money, but also to have two coats. He said to the rich young man that he could not enter into the kingdom of God because he was rich, and that it is easier for a camel to go through the needle's eye than for a rich man to enter the kingdom of God.

He said that he who would not leave every thing—his houses and children and his fields—in order to follow him, was not his disciple. He spoke a parable about a rich man who had done nothing wrong (like our own rich people), but merely dressed well and ate and drank well, yet by this lost his own soul; and about a beggar named Lazarus, who had done nothing good, but who had saved his soul by his beggar's life.

This truth had long been known to me; but the false teaching of the world had so cunningly hidden it that it became a theory in the sense which men like to attach to this word,—that is, a pure abstraction. But as soon as I succeeded in pulling down in my consciousness the sophistry of the world's teaching, then theory became one with practice and the reality of my life and the life of all men became its unavoidable result.

I came to understand that man, besides living for his own good, must work for the good of others; and that if we were to draw our comparison from the world of animals, as some men are so fond of doing in justifying violence and contest by the law of the struggle for existence, we must take this comparison from the lives of social animals like bees; and therefore man, to say nothing of that love to his neighbours which is incumbent on him, is called upon to serve his fellows and their common object, as much by reason as by his very nature.

I understood that this is the natural law of man, by fulfilling which he can alone fulfil his calling and therefore be happy. I understood that this law has been and is being violated by the fact that men (as robber-bees do) free themselves from labour by violence, and utilize the labour of others, using this labour not for the common purpose but for the personal satisfaction of their constantly increasing lusts, and also, like robber-bees, they perish thereby. I understood that the misfortune of men comes from the slavery in which some men are kept by others; and I understood that this slavery is brought about in our days by military force, violence, by the appropriation of land, and by the exaction of money.

And, having understood the meaning of all these three instruments of modern slavery, I could not help desiring to free myself from any share in it.

When I was a landlord, possessing serfs, and came to understand the immorality of such a position, I, along with other men who had understood the same thing, tried to free myself from it. And I freed myself from this state thus. Finding it immoral, but not being able as yet to free myself wholly from it, I tried meanwhile to assert my rights as a serf-owner as little as possible.

I cannot help doing the same now with reference to the present slavery—that is, I try as little as possible to assert my claims while I am unable to free myself from the power which gives me land-ownership, and from money raised by the violence of military force—and at the same time by all means in my power to suggest to other men the unlawfulness and inhumanity of these imaginary rights.

The share in enslaving men consists, on the standpoint of a slave-owner, in utilizing the labour of others. (It is all the same whether the enslaving is based on a claim to the person of the slave or on the possession of land or money.) And, therefore, if a man really does not like slavery and does not desire to be a partaker in it, the first thing which he must do is this: neither take men's labour by serving the government, nor possess land or money.

The refusal of all the means in use for taking another's labour will unavoidably bring such a man to the necessity of lessening his wants on the one hand, and, on the other, of doing himself what formerly was done for him by other men. This simple and unavoidable conclusion enters into every detail of my life, changes it entirely, and at once sets me free from the moral sufferings I had endured at the sight of the misery and wickedness of men.

The first cause was the accumulation of people in towns, and the absorption there of the products of the country.

All that a man needs is not to desire to take another's labour by serving the government and possessing land and money, and then, according to his strength and ability, to satisfy unaided his own wants. The idea of leaving his village would never enter the mind of such a man, because in the country it is easier for him to satisfy his wants personally, while in a town everything is the product of the labour of others, all must be bought; in the country a man will always be able to help the needy, and will not experience that feeling of being useless, which I felt in the town when I wanted to help men, not with my own, but with other men's labours.

The second cause was the estrangement between the poor and the rich. A man need only not desire to profit by other men's labour by serving the government and possessing land and money, and he would be compelled to satisfy his wants himself, and at once involuntarily that barrier would be pushed down which separates him from the working-people, and he would be one with the people, standing shoulder to shoulder with them, and seeing the possibility of helping them.

The third cause was shame, based on the consciousness of the immorality of possessing money with which I wanted to help others. A man need only not desire to profit by another man's labour by serving the government and possessing land and money, and he will never have that superfluous "fool's money," the fact of possessing which made those who wanted money ask me for pecuniary assistance which I was not able to satisfy, and called forth in me the consciousness of my unrighteousness.

CHAPTER XXIII

I saw that the cause of the sufferings and depravity of men lies in the fact that some men are in bondage to others; and therefore I came to the obvious conclusion that if I want to help men I have first of all to leave off causing those very misfortunes which I want to remedy,—in other words, I must not share in the enslaving of men.

I was led to the enslaving of men by the circumstance that from my infancy I had been accustomed not to work, but to profit by the labour of others, and that I had been living in a society which is not only accustomed to this slavery but which justifies it by all kinds of sophistry, clever and foolish.

I came to the following simple conclusion, that, in order to avoid causing the sufferings and depravity of men, I ought to make other men work for me as little as possible and to work myself as much as possible.

It was by this roundabout way that I arrived at the inevitable conclusion to which the Chinese arrived some thousand years ago, and which they express thus: "If there is one idle man, there must be another who is starving."

I came to this simple and natural conclusion, that if I pity the exhausted horse on whose back I ride the first thing for me to do if I really pity him is to get off his back and walk. This answer, which gives such complete satisfaction to the moral sense, had always been before my eyes, as it is before the eyes of every one, but we do not all see it, and look aside.

In seeking to heal our social diseases we look everywhere,—to the governmental, anti-governmental, scientific, and philanthropic superstitions,—and yet we do not see that which meets the eyes of every one. We fill our drains with filth and require other men to clean them, and pretend to be very sorry for them and want to ease their work; and we invent all sorts of devices except one, the simplest; namely, that we should ourselves remove our slops so long as we find it necessary to produce them in our rooms.

For him who really suffers from the sufferings of the other men surrounding him, there exists a most clear, simple, and easy means, the only one sufficient to heal this evil and to confer a sense of the lawfulness of one's life. This means is that which John the Baptist recommended when he answered the question, "What shall we do then?" and which was confirmed by Christ: not to have more than one coat, and not to possess money,—that is, not to profit by another man's labour. And in order not to profit by another's labour, we must do with our own hands all that we can do. This is so plain and simple! But it is plain and simple and clear only when our wants are also plain, and when we ourselves are still sound and not corrupted to the backbone by idleness and laziness.

I live in a village, lie by the stove, and tell my neighbour, who is my debtor, to chop wood and light the stove. It is obvious that I am lazy and take my neighbour away from his own work; and at last I feel ashamed of it; and besides, it grows dull for me to be always lying down when my muscles are strong and accustomed to work,—and I go to chop the wood myself.

But slavery of all kinds has been going on so long, so many artificial wants have grown about it, so many people with different degrees of familiarity with these wants are interwoven with one another, through so many generations men have been spoiled and made effeminate, such complicated temptations and justifications of luxury and idleness have been invented by men, that for one who stands on the top of the pyramid of idle men, it is not at all so easy to understand his sin as it is for the peasant who compels his neighbour to light his stove.

Men who stand at the top find it most difficult to understand what is required of them. From the height of the structure of lies on which they stand they become giddy when they look at that spot on the earth to which they must descend in order to begin to live, not righteously, but only not quite inhumanly; and that is why this plain and clear truth appears to these men so strange.

A man who employs ten servants in livery, coachmen and cooks, who has pictures and pianos, must certainly regard as strange and even ridiculous the simple preliminary duty of, I do not say a good man, but of every man who is not an animal, to hew that wood with which his food is cooked and by which he is warmed; to clean those boots in which he carelessly stepped into the mud; to bring that water with which he keeps himself clean; and to carry away those slops in which he has washed himself.

But besides the estrangement of men from the truth, there is another cause which hinders them from seeing the duty of doing the most simple and natural physical work; that is the complication and intermingling of the conditions in which a rich man lives.

This morning I entered the corridor in which the stoves are heated. A peasant was heating the stove which warmed my son's room. I entered his bedroom: he was asleep, and it was eleven o'clock in the morning. The excuse was, "To-day is a holiday; no lessons." A stout lad of eighteen years of age, having over-eaten himself the previous night, is sleeping until eleven o'clock; and a peasant of his own age, who had already that morning done a quantity of work, was now lighting the tenth stove. "It would be better, perhaps, if the peasant did not light the stove to warm this stout, lazy fellow!" thought I; but I remembered at once that this stove also warmed the room of our housekeeper, a woman of forty years of age, who had been working the night before till three o'clock in the morning to prepare everything for the supper which my son ate; and then she put away the dishes, and, notwithstanding this, got up at seven. She cannot heat the stove herself: she has no time for that. The peasant is heating the stove for her, too. And under her name my lazy fellow was being warmed.

True, the advantages are all interwoven; but without much consideration the conscience of each will say, On whose side is the labour, and on whose the idleness? But not only does conscience tell this, the account-book also tells it: the more money one spends, the more people work for us. The less one spends, the more one works one's self. "My luxurious life gives means of living to others. Where should my old footman go, if I were to discharge him?" "What! every one must do everything for himself? Make his coat as well as hew his wood? And how about division of labour? And industry and social undertakings?" And, last of all, come the most horrible of words,—civilization, science, art!

CHAPTER XXIV

Last March I was returning home late in the evening. On turning into a bye-lane I perceived on the snow in a distant field some black shadows. I should not have noticed this but for the policeman who stood at the end of the lane and cried in the direction of the shadows, "Vasili, why don't you come along?"

"She won't move," answered a voice; and thereupon the shadows came towards the policeman. I stopped and asked him,—

"What is the matter?"

He said, "We have got some girls from Rzhanoff's house, and are taking them to the police-station; and one of them lags behind, and won't come along."

A night-watchman in sheepskin coat appeared now driving on a girl who slouched along while he prodded her from behind. I, the watchman and the policeman, were wearing winter coats: she alone had none, having only her gown on. In the dark I could distinguish only a brown dress and a kerchief round her head and neck. She was short, like most starvelings, and had a broad, clumsy figure.

"We aren't going to stay here all night for you, you hag! Get on, or I'll give it you!" shouted the policeman. He was evidently fatigued and tired of her. She walked some paces and stopped again.

The old watchman, a good-natured man (I knew him), pulled her by the hand. "I'll wake you up! come along!" said he, pretending to be angry. She staggered, and began to speak with a croaking hoarse voice, "Let me be; don't you push. I'll get on myself."

"You'll be frozen to death," he returned.

"A girl like me won't be frozen: I've lots of hot blood."

She meant it as a joke, but her words sounded like a curse. By a lamp, which stood not far from the gate of my house, she stopped again, leaned back against the paling, and began to seek for something among her petticoats with awkward, frozen hands. They again shouted to her; but she only muttered and continued searching. She held in one hand a crumpled cigarette and matches in the other. I remained behind her: I was ashamed to pass by or to stay and look at her. But I made up my mind and came up to her. She leaned with her shoulder against the paling and vainly tried to light a match on it.

I looked narrowly at her face. She was indeed a starveling and appeared to me to be a woman of about thirty. Her complexion was dirty; her eyes small, dim, and bleared with drinking; she had a squat nose; her lips were wry and slavering, with downcast angles; from under her kerchief fell a tuft of dry hair. Her figure was long and flat; her arms and legs short.

I stopped in front of her. She looked at me and grinned as if she knew all that I was thinking about. I felt that I ought to say something to her. I wanted to show her that I pitied her.

"Have you parents?" I asked. She laughed hoarsely, then suddenly stopped, and, lifting her brows, began to look at me steadfastly.

"Have you parents?" I repeated.

She smiled with a grimace which seemed to say, "What a question for him to put!"

"I have a mother," she said at last; "but what's that to you?"

"And how old are you?"

"I am over fifteen," she said, at once answering a question she was accustomed to hear.

"Come, come! go on; we shall all be frozen for you, the deuce take you!" shouted the policeman; and she edged off from the paling and staggered along the lane to the police-station: and I turned to the gate and entered my house, and asked whether my daughters were at home. I was told that they had been to an evening party, had enjoyed themselves much, and now were asleep.

The next morning I was about to go to the police-station to enquire what had become of this unhappy girl. I was ready to start early enough, when one of those unfortunate men called, who from weakness have dropped out of the gentlemanly line of life to which they have been accustomed, and who rise and fall by turns. I had been acquainted with him three years. During this time he had several times sold every thing he had,—even his clothes; and, having just done so again, he passed his nights temporarily in Rzhanoff's house, and his days at my lodgings. He met me as I was going out, and, without listening to me, began at once to relate what had happened at Rzhanoff's house the night before.

He began to relate it, yet had not got through one-half when, all of a sudden, he, an old man, who had gone through much in his life, began to sob, and, ceasing to speak, turned his face away from me. This was what he related. I ascertained the truth of his story on the spot, where I learned some new particulars, which I shall relate too.

A washerwoman thirty years of age, fair, quiet, good-looking, but delicate, passed her nights in the same lodging-house, the ground-floor of No. 32 where my friend slept among various shifting night-lodgers, men and women, who for five kopeks slept with each other.

The landlady at this lodging was the mistress of a boatman. In summer her lover kept a boat; and in winter they earned their living by letting lodgings to night-lodgers at three kopeks without a pillow, and at five kopeks with one.

The washerwoman had been living here some months, and was a quiet woman; but lately they began to object to her because she coughed, and prevented the other lodgers from sleeping. An old woman in particular, eighty years old, half silly, and a permanent inmate of this lodging, began to dislike the washerwoman and kept annoying her because she disturbed her sleep; for all night she coughed like a sheep.

The washerwoman said nothing. She owed for rent, and felt herself guilty, and was therefore compelled to endure. She began to work less and less, for her strength failed her; and that was why she was unable to pay her rent. She had not been to work at all the whole of the last week; and she had been making the lives of all, and particularly of the old woman, miserable by her cough.

Four days ago the landlady gave her notice to leave. She already owed sixty kopeks, and could not pay them, and there was no hope of doing so; and other lodgers complained of her cough.

When the landlady gave the washerwoman notice, and told her she must go away if she did not pay the rent, the old woman was glad, and pushed her out into the yard. The washerwoman went away, but came back again in an hour, and the landlady had not the heart to send her away again.... During the second and the third day the landlady left her there. "Where shall I go?" she kept saying. On the third day the landlady's lover, a Moscow man, who knew all the rules and regulations, went for a policeman. The policeman, with a sword and a pistol slung on a red cord, came into the lodging and quietly and politely turned the washerwoman out into the street.

It was a bright, sunny, but frosty day in March. The melting snow ran down in streams, the house-porters were breaking the ice. The hackney sledges bumped on the ice-glazed snow, and creaked over the stones. The washerwoman went up the hill on the sunny side, got to the church, and sat down in the sun at the church-porch. But when the sun began to go down behind the houses and the pools of water began to be covered with a thin sheet of ice, the washerwoman felt chilly and terrified. She got up and slowly walked on.... Where? Home,—to the only house in which she had been living lately.

While she was walking there, several times resting herself, it began to get dark. She approached the gate, turned into it, her foot slipped, she gave a shriek, and fell down.

One man passed by, then another. "She must be drunk," they thought. Another man passed, and stumbled up against her, and said to the house-porter, "Some tipsy woman is lying at the gate. I very nearly broke my neck over her. Won't you take her away?"

The house-porter came. The washerwoman was dead. This was what my friend related to me.

The reader will perhaps fancy I have picked out particular cases in the prostitute of fifteen years of age and the story of this washerwoman; but let him not think so: this really happened in one and the same night. I do not exactly remember the date, only it was in March, 1884.

Having heard my friend's story I went to the police-station, intending from there to go to Rzhanoff's house to learn all the particulars of the washerwoman's story.

The weather was fine and sunny; and again under the ice of the previous night, in the shade, you could see the water running; and in the sun, in the square, everything was melting fast. The trees of the garden appeared blue from over the river; the sparrows that were reddish in winter, and unnoticed then, now attracted people's attention by their merriness; men also tried to be merry, but they all had too many cares. The bells of the churches sounded; and blending with them were heard sounds of shooting from the barracks,—the hiss of the rifle balls, and the crack when they struck the target.

I entered the police-station. There some armed men—policemen—led me to their chief. He, also armed with a sword, sabre, and pistol, was busy giving some orders about a ragged, trembling old man who was standing before him, and from weakness could not clearly answer what was asked of him. Having done with the old man, he turned to me. I inquired about the prostitute of last night. He first listened to me attentively, then he smiled, not only because I did not know why they were taken to the police-station, but more particularly at my astonishment at her youth. "Goodness! there are some of twelve, thirteen, and fourteen years of age often," said he, in a lively tone.

To my question about the girl of yesterday, he told me that she had probably been already sent to the committee (if I understood him right). To my question where such women passed the night, he gave a vague answer. The one about whom I spoke he did not remember. There were so many of them every day.

At Rzhanoff's house, in No. 32, I already found the sacristan reading prayers over the dead washerwoman. She had been brought in and laid on her former pallet; and the lodgers, all starvelings themselves, contributed money for the prayers, the coffin, and the shroud; the old woman had dressed her, and laid her out. The clerk was reading something in the dark; a woman in a cloak stood holding a wax taper; and with a similar wax taper stood a man (a gentleman, it is fair to state), in a nice great-coat, trimmed with an astrachan collar, in bright goloshes, and with a starched shirt. That was her brother. He had been hunted up.

I passed by the dead woman to the landlady's room in order to ask her all the particulars. She was afraid of my questions,—afraid probably of being charged with something; but by and by she grew talkative and told me all. On passing by again, I looked at the dead body. All the dead are beautiful; but this one was particularly beautiful and touching in her coffin, with her clear, pale face, with closed, prominent eyes, sunken cheeks, and fair, soft hair over her high forehead; her face looked weary, but kind, and not sad at all, but rather astonished. And indeed, if the living do not see, the dead may well be astonished.

On the day I wrote this there was a great ball in Moscow. On the same night I left home after eight o'clock. I live in a locality surrounded by factories; and I left home after the factory whistle had sounded, and when, after a week of incessant work, the people were freed for their holiday. Factory-men passed by me, and I by them, all turning their steps to the public-houses and inns. Many were already tipsy: many were with women.

Every morning at five I hear each of the whistles, which means that the labour of women, children, and old people has begun. At eight o'clock another whistle,—this means half an hour's rest; at twelve the third whistle,—this means an hour for dinner. At eight o'clock the fourth whistle, indicating cessation from work. By a strange coincidence, all the three factories in my neighbourhood produce only the articles necessary for balls.

In one factory,—the one nearest to me,—they make nothing but stockings; in the other opposite, silk stuffs; in the third, perfumes and pomades.

One may, on hearing these whistles, attach to them no other meaning than that of the indication of time. "There, the whistle has sounded: it is time to go out for a walk."

But one may associate with them also the meaning they have in reality,—that at the first whistle at five o'clock in the morning, men and women, who have slept side by side in a damp cellar, get up in the dark, and hurry away into the noisy building to take their part in a work of which they see neither cessation nor utility for themselves, and work often so in the heat, in suffocating exhalations, with very rare intervals of rest, for one, two, or three, or even twelve or more hours. They fall asleep, and get up again, and again do this work, meaningless for themselves, to which they are goaded only by want. So it goes on from one week to another, interrupted only by holidays.

And now I see these working-people freed for one of these holidays. They go out into the street: everywhere there are inns, public-houses, and gay women. And they, in a drunken state, pull each other by the arms, and carry along with them girls like the one whom I saw conducted to the police-station: they hire hackney-coaches, and ride and walk from one inn to another, and abuse each other, and totter about, and say they know not what.

Formerly when I saw the factory people knocking about in this way I used to turn aside with disgust, and almost reproached them; but since I hear these daily whistles, and know what they mean, I am only astonished that all these men do not come into the condition of the utter beggars with whom Moscow is filled, and the women into the position of the girl whom I had met near my house.

Thus I walked on, looking at these men, observing how they went about the streets, till eleven o'clock. Then their movements became quieter: there remained here and there a few tipsy people, and I met some men and women who were being conducted to the police-station. And now, from every side, carriages appeared, all going in one direction. On the coach-box sat a coachman, sometimes in a sheepskin coat, and a footman,—a dandy with a cockade. Well-fed horses, covered with cloth, trotted at the rate of fifteen miles an hour. In the carriages sat ladies wrapped in shawls, taking great care not to spoil their flowers and their toilets. All, beginning with the harness on the horses, the carriages, indiarubber wheels, the cloth of the coachman's coat, down to the stockings, shoes, flowers, velvet, gloves, scents,—all these articles have been made by those men, some of whom fell asleep on their own pallets in their mean rooms, some in night-houses with prostitutes, and others in the police-station.

The ball-goers drive past these men, in and with things made by them; and it does not even enter into their minds that there could possibly be any connection between the ball they are going to, and these tipsy people to whom their coachmen shout out so angrily. With easy minds and assurance that they are doing nothing wrong, but something very good, they enjoy themselves at the ball.

Enjoy themselves!

From eleven o'clock in the evening till six in the morning, in the very depth of the night; while with empty stomachs men are lying in night-lodgings, or dying as the washer-woman had done!

The enjoyment of the ball consists in women and girls uncovering their bosoms, putting on artificial protuberances at the back, and altogether getting themselves up as no girl and no woman who is not yet depraved would, on any account, appear before men; and in this half-naked condition, with uncovered bosoms, and arms bare up to the shoulders, with dresses puffed behind and tight round the hips, in the brightest light, women and girls, whose first virtue has always been modesty, appear among strange men, who are also dressed in indecently tight-fitting clothes, embrace each other, and pivot round and round to the sound of exciting music. Old women, often also half naked like the younger ones, are sitting looking on, and eating and drinking:

the old men do the same. No wonder it is done at night when everyone else is sleeping, so that no one may see it!

But it is not done at night in order to hide it; there is nothing indeed to hide; all is very nice and good; and by this enjoyment, in which is swallowed up the painful labour of thousands, not only is nobody harmed, but by this very thing poor people are fed!

The ball goes on very merrily, may be, but how did it come to do so? When we see in society or among ourselves one who has not eaten, or is cold, we are ashamed to enjoy ourselves, and cannot begin to be merry until he is fed, to say nothing of the fact that we cannot even imagine that there are people who can enjoy themselves by means of anything which produces the sufferings of others.

We are disgusted with and do not understand the enjoyment of brutal boys who have squeezed a dog's tail into a piece of split wood. How is it, then, that in our enjoyment we become blind, and do not see the cleft in which we have pinched those men who suffer for our enjoyment.

We know that each woman at this ball whose dress costs a hundred and fifty rubles was not born at the ball, but has lived in the country, has seen peasants, is acquainted with a nurse and maid whose fathers and brothers are poor, for whom the earning of a hundred and fifty rubles to build a cottage with is the end and aim of a long, laborious life. She knows all this; how can she, then, enjoy herself, knowing that on her half-naked body she is wearing the cottage which is the dream of her housemaid's brother?

But let us suppose she has not thought about this: still she cannot help knowing that velvet and silk, sweetmeats and flowers, and laces and dresses, do not grow of themselves, but are made by men. One would think she could not help knowing that men make all these things, and under what circumstances, and why. She cannot help knowing that her dressmaker, whom she scolded to-day, made this dress not at all out of love to her, therefore she cannot help knowing that all these things—her laces, flowers, and velvet—were made from sheer want.

But perhaps she is so blinded that she does not think of this. Well, but, at all events, she could not help knowing that five people, old, respectable, often delicate men and women, have not slept all night, and have been busy on her account. She saw their tired, gloomy faces. This, also, she could not help knowing,—that on this night there were twenty-eight degrees of frost, and that her coachman—an old man—was sitting in this frost all night on his coach-box.

But I know that they do not really see this. If from the hypnotic influence of the ball these young women and girls fail to see all this, we cannot judge them. Poor things! They consider all to be good which is pronounced so by their elders. How do these elders explain their cruelty? They, indeed, always answer in the same way: "I compel no one; what I have, I have bought; footmen, chambermaids, coachman, I hire. There is no harm in engaging and in buying. I compel none; I hire; what wrong is there in that?"

Some days ago I called on a friend. Passing through the first room I wondered at seeing two women at a table, for I knew my acquaintance was a bachelor. A skinny yellow, old-looking woman, about thirty, with a kerchief thrown over her shoulders, was briskly doing something over the table with her hands, jerking nervously, as if in a fit. Opposite to her sat a young girl, who was also doing something and jerking in the same way. They both seemed to be suffering from St. Vitus's dance. I came nearer and looked closer to see what they were about.

They glanced up at me and then continued their work as attentively as before.

Before them were spread tobacco and cigarettes. They were making cigarettes. The woman rubbed the tobacco fine between the palms of her hands, caught it up by a machine, put on the tubes, and threw them to the girl. The girl folded the papers, put them over the cigarette, threw it aside, and took up another.

All this was performed with such speed, with such dexterity, that it was impossible to describe it. I expressed my wonder at their quickness. "I have been at this business fourteen years," said the woman.

"Is it hard work?"

"Yes: my chest aches, and the air is choky with tobacco."

But it was not necessary for her to have said so: you need only have looked at her or at the girl. The latter had been at this business three years; but anyone not seeing her at this work would have said that she had a strong constitution which was already beginning to be broken.

My acquaintance, a kind-hearted man of liberal views, hired these women to make him cigarettes at two rubles and a half (5s.) a thousand. He has money, and he pays it away for this work: what harm is there in it?

My acquaintance gets up at twelve. His evenings, from six to two, he spends at cards or at the piano; he eats and drinks well; other people do all the work for him. He has devised for himself a new pleasure,—smoking. I can remember when he began to smoke. Here are a woman and a girl who can scarcely earn their living by transforming themselves into machines, and who pass all their lives in breathing tobacco, thus ruining their lives. He has money which he has not earned, and he prefers playing at cards to making cigarettes for himself. He gives these women money only on condition that they continue to live as miserably as they lived before in making cigarettes for him.

I am fond of cleanliness; and I give money on condition that the washerwoman washes my shirts, which I change twice a day; and the washing of these shirts having taxed the utmost strength of the washerwoman, she has died.

What is wrong in this?

Men who buy and hire will continue doing so whether I do or do not; they will force other people to make velvets and dainties, and will buy them whether I do or do not; so also they will hire people to make cigarettes and to wash shirts. Why should I, then, deprive myself of velvets, sweetmeats, cigarettes, and clean shirts, when their production is already set in going. Often,—almost constantly I hear this reasoning.

This is the very reasoning which a crowd, maddened with the passion of destruction, will employ. It is the same reasoning which leads a pack of dogs, when one of their number runs against another and knocks it down, the rest attack it and tear it to pieces. Others have already begun, have done a little mischief; why shouldn't I, too, do the same? What can it possibly signify if I wear a dirty shirt and make my cigarettes myself? could that help any one? men ask who desire to justify themselves.

Had we not wandered so far from truth one would be ashamed to answer this question; but we are so entangled that such a question seems natural to us, and, therefore, though I feel ashamed, I must answer it.

What difference would it be if I should wear my shirt a week instead of a day, and make my cigarettes myself, or leave off smoking altogether?

The difference would be this,—that a certain washerwoman, and a certain cigarette-maker, would exert themselves less, and what I gave formerly for the washing of my shirt, and for the making of my cigarettes, I may give now to that or to another woman; and working-people who are tired by their work, instead of overworking themselves, will be able to rest and to have tea. But I have heard objections to this, so ashamed are the rich and luxurious to understand their position.

They reply, "If I should wear dirty linen, leave off smoking, and give this money away to the poor, then this money would be all the same taken away from them, and my drop will not help to swell the sea."

I am still more ashamed to answer such a reply, but at the same time I must do so. If I came among savages who gave me chops which I thought delicious, but the next day I learned (perhaps saw myself) that these delicious chops were made of a human prisoner who had been slain in order to make them; and if I think it bad to eat men, however delicious the cutlets may be, and however general the custom to eat men among the persons with whom I live, and however small the utility of my refusal to eat them may be,—to the prisoners who have been prepared for food,—I shall not and cannot eat them.

It may be that I shall eat human flesh when urged by hunger; but I shall not make a feast of it, and shall not take part in feasts with human flesh, and shall not seek such feasts, nor be proud of my partaking of them.

CHAPTER XXV

But what is to be done, then? We did not do it, did we? And if not we, who did?

We say, "It is not we who have done all this; it has been done of itself"; as children say when they break anything, that "it broke itself." We say that, as towns are already in existence, we, who are living there, must feed men by buying their labour. But that is not true. It need only be observed how we live in the country, and how we feed people there.

Winter is over: Easter is coming. In the town the same orgies of the rich go on,—on the boulevards, in gardens, in the parks, on the river; music, theatres, riding, illuminations, fire-works. But in the country it is still better,—the air is purer; the trees, the meadows, the flowers, are fresher. We must go where all is budding and blooming. And now we, the majority of rich people, who live by other men's labour, go into the country to breathe the purer air, to look at the meadows and woods. Here in the country among humble villagers who feed on bread and onions, work eighteen hours every day, and have neither sufficient sleep nor clothes, rich people take up their abode. No one tempts these people: here are no factories, and no idle hands, of which there are so many in town, whom we may imagine we feed by giving them work to do. Here people never can do their own work in time during the summer; and not only are there no idle hands, but much property is lost for want of hands; and an immense number of men, children, and old people, and women with child, overwork themselves.

How, then, do rich people order their lives here in the country? Thus: if there happens to be an old mansion, built in the time of the serfs, then this house is renovated and re-decorated: if there is not, one is built of two or three stories. The rooms, which are from twelve to twenty and more in number, are all about sixteen feet high. The floors are inlaid; in the windows are put whole panes of glass, costly carpets on the floors; expensive furniture is procured,—a sideboard, for instance, costing from twenty to sixty pounds. Near the mansion, roads are made; flower-beds are laid out; there are croquet-lawns, giant-strides, reflecting globes, conservatories, and hot-houses, and always luxurious stables. All is painted in colours, prepared with the very oil which the old people and children lack for their porridge. If a rich man can afford it he buys such a house for himself; if he cannot he hires one: but however poor and however liberal a man of our circle may be, he always takes up his abode in the country in such a house, for building and keeping which it is necessary to take away dozens of working-people who have not enough time to do their own business in the field to earn their living.

Here we cannot say that factories are already in existence and will continue so whether we make use of their work or no; we cannot say that we are feeding idle hands; here we plainly establish the factories for making things necessary for us, and simply make use of the surrounding people; we divert the people from work necessary for them, as for us and for all, and by such system deprave some, and ruin the lives and the health of others.

There lives, let us say, in a village, an educated and respectable family of the upper class, or that of a government officer. All its members and the visitors assemble towards the middle of June, because up to June they had been studying and passing their examinations: they assemble when mowing begins, and they stay until September, until the harvest and sowing time. The members of the family (as almost all men of this class) remain in the country from the beginning of the urgent work,—hay-making,—not to the end of it, indeed, because in September the sowing goes on, and the digging up of potatoes, but till labour begins to slacken. During the whole time of the stay, around them and close by the peasants' summer work has been proceeding, the strain of which, however much we may have heard or read of it, however much we may have looked at it, we can form no adequate idea without having experienced it ourselves.

The members of the family, about ten persons have been living as they did in town, if possible still worse than in town, because here in the village they are supposed to be resting (after doing nothing), and offer no pretence in the way of work, and no excuse for their idleness.

In the midsummer-lent, when people are forced from want to feed on kvas and bread and onions, begins the mowing time. Gentlefolk who live in the country see this labour, partly order it, partly admire it; enjoy the smell of the drying hay, the sound of women's songs, the noise of the scythes, and the sight of the rows of mowers, and of the women raking. They see this near their house as well as when they, with young people and children who do nothing all the day long, drive well-fed horses a distance of a few hundred yards to the bathing-place.

The work of mowing is one of the most important in the world. Nearly every year, from want of hands and of time, the meadows remain half uncut and may remain so till the rains begin; so that the degree of intensity of the labour decides the question whether twenty or more per cent will be added to the stores of the world, or whether this hay will be left to rot or spoil while yet uncut.

And if there is more hay, there will be also more meat for old people and milk for children; thus matters stand in general; but in particular for each mower here is decided the question of bread and milk for himself, and for his children during the winter.

Each of the working-people, male and female, knows this: even the children know that this is an important business and that one ought to work with all one's strength, carry a jug with kvas for the father to the mowing-place, and, shifting it from one hand to another, run barefoot as quickly as possible, a distance of perhaps a mile and a half from the village, in order to be in time for dinner, that father may not grumble. Every one knows, that, from the mowing to the harvest, there will be no cessation of labour, and no time for rest. And besides mowing, each has some other business to do,—to plough up new land and harrow it; the women have the linen to make, bread to bake, and the washing to do; and the peasants must drive to the mill and to market; they have the official affairs of their community to attend to; they have also to provide the local government officials with means of locomotion, and to pass the night in the fields with the pastured horses.

All, old and young and sick, work with all their strength.

The peasants work in such a way, that, when cutting the last rows, the mowers, some of them weak people, growing youths, and old men, are so tired, that, having rested a little, it is with great pain they begin anew; the women, often with child, work hard too.

It is a strained, incessant labour. All work to the utmost of their strength, and use not only all their provisions but what they have in store. During harvest-time all the peasants grow thinner although they never were very stout.

There is a small company labouring in the hayfield; three peasants—one an old man, another his married nephew, and the third the village cobbler, a thin, wiry man. Their mowing this morning decides their fate for the coming winter, whether they will be able to keep a cow and pay their taxes. This is their second weeks' work. The rain hindered them for a while. After the rain had left off and the water had dried up they decided to make hayricks; and in order to do it quicker they decided that two women must rake to each scythe. With the old man came out his wife, fifty years of age, worn out with labour and the bearing of eleven children; deaf, but still strong enough for work; and his daughter, thirteen years of age, a short but brisk and strong little girl.

With the nephew came his wife,—a tall woman, as strong as a peasant, and his sister in law,—a soldier's wife, who was with child. With the cobbler came his wife,—a strong working-woman, and her mother,—an old woman about eighty, who for the rest of the year used to beg.

They all draw up in a line, and work from morning to evening in the burning sun of June. It is steaming hot and a thunder-shower is threatening. Every moment of work is precious. They have not wished to leave off working even to fetch water or kvas. A small boy, the grandson of the old woman, brings them water. The old woman is evidently anxious only on one point,—not to be sent away from work. She does not let the rake out of her hands, and moves about with great difficulty. The little boy, quite bent under the jug with water, heavier than himself, walks with short steps on his bare feet, and carries the jug with many shifts. The little girl takes on her shoulders a load of hay which is also heavier than herself; walks a few paces, and stops, then throws it down, having no strength to carry it farther. The old man's wife rakes together unceasingly, her kerchief loosened from her disordered hair; she carries the hay, breathing heavily and staggering under the burden: the cobbler's mother is only raking, but this is also beyond her strength; she slowly drags her feet, in baste shoes, and looks gloomily before her, like one very ill, or at the point of death. The old man purposely sends her far away from the others, to rake about the ricks, in order that she may not attempt to compete with them; but she does not leave off working, but continues with the same dead gloomy face as long as the others.

The sun is already setting behind the wood and the ricks are not yet in order: there is much still to be done.

All feel that it is time to leave off working but no one says so; each waiting for the other to suggest it. At last, the cobbler, realizing that he has no more strength left, proposes to the old man to leave the ricks till to-morrow, and the old man agrees to it; and at once the women go to fetch their clothes, their jugs, their pitchforks; and the old woman sits down where she was standing, and then lays herself down with the same fixed stare on her face. But as the women go away she gets up groaning, and, crawling along, follows them.

Let us turn to the country-house. The same evening, when from the side of the village were heard the rattle of the scythes of the toil-worn mowers who were returning from work, the sounds of the hammer against the anvil, the cries of women and girls who had just had time to put away their rakes, and were already running to drive the cattle in,—with those blend other sounds from the country-house. Rattle, rattle, goes the piano; a Hungarian song is heard through the noise of the croquet-balls; before the stable an open carriage is standing harnessed with four fat horses, which has been hired for twenty shillings to bring some guests a distance of ten miles.

Horses standing by the carriage rattle their little bells. Before them hay has been thrown, which they are scattering with their hoofs, the same hay which the peasants have been gathering with such hard labour. In the yard of this mansion there is movement; a healthy, well-fed fellow in a pink shirt, presented to him for his service as a house-porter, is calling the coachmen and telling them to harness and saddle some horses. Two peasants who live here as coachmen come out of their room, and go in an easy manner, swinging their arms, to saddle horses for the ladies and gentlemen. Still nearer to the house the sounds of another piano are heard. It is the music-mistress,—who lives in the family to teach the children,—practising her Schumann. The sounds of one piano jangle with those of another. Quite near the house walk two nurses; one is young, another old; they lead and carry children to bed; these children are of the same age as those who ran from the village with jugs. One nurse is English: she cannot speak Russian. She was engaged to come from England, not from being distinguished by some peculiar qualities but simply because she does not speak Russian. Farther on is another person, a French woman, who is also engaged because she does not know Russian. Farther on a peasant, with two women, is watering flowers near the house: another is cleaning a gun for one of the young gentlemen. Here two women are carrying a basket with clean linen,—they have been washing for all these gentlefolks. In the house two women have scarcely time to wash the plates and dishes after the company, who have just done eating; and two peasants in evening clothes are running up and down the stairs, serving coffee, tea, wine, seltzer-water, etc. Up-stairs a table is spread. One meal has just ended, and another will soon begin, to continue till cock-crow and often till morning dawns. Some are sitting smoking, playing cards; others are sitting and smoking, engaged in discussing liberal ideas of reform; and others, again, walk to and fro, eat, smoke, and, not knowing what to do, have made up their mind to take a drive.

The household consists of fifteen persons, healthy men and women; and thirty persons, healthy working-people, male and female, labour for them. And this takes place there, where every hour, and each little boy, are precious.

This will be so, also, in July, when the peasants, not having had their sleep out, will mow the oats at night in order that it may not be lost, and the women will get up before dawn in order to finish their threshing in time; when this old woman, who had been exhausted during the harvest, and the women with child, and the little children will again all overwork themselves, and when there is a great want of hands, horses, carts, in order to house this corn upon which all men feed, of which millions of bushels are necessary in Russia in order that men should not die: during even such a time, the idle lives of ladies and gentlemen will go on. There will be private theatricals, picnics, hunting, drinking, eating, piano-playing, singing, dancing,—in fact, incessant orgies.

Here, at least, it is impossible to find any excuse from the fact that all this had been going on before: nothing of the kind had been in existence. We ourselves carefully create such a life, taking bread and labour away from the work-worn people. We live sumptuously, as if there were no connection whatever between the dying washerwoman, child-prostitute, women worn out by making cigarettes and all the intense labour around us to which their unnourished strength is inadequate. We do not want to see the fact that if there were not our idle, luxurious, depraved lives, there would not be this labour, disproportioned to the strength of people, and that if there were not this labour we could not go on living in the same way.

It appears to us that their sufferings are one thing and our lives another, and that we, living as we do, are innocent and pure as doves. We read the description of the lives of the Romans, and wonder at the inhumanity of a heartless Lucullus, who gorged himself with fine dishes and delicious wines while people were starving: we shake our heads and wonder at the barbarism of our grandfathers,—the serf-owners,—who provided themselves with orchestras and theatres, and employed whole villages to keep up their gardens. From the height of our greatness we wonder at their inhumanity. We read the words of Isaiah v., 8:

"Woe unto them that join house to house, that lay field to field, till there be no room, and ye be made to dwell alone in the midst of the land.

Woe unto them that rise up early in the morning, that they may follow strong drink; that tarry late into the night, till wine inflame them!

The harp, and the lute, the tabret, the pipe, and wine are in their feasts: but they regard not the work of the Lord, neither have they considered the operation of his hands.

Woe unto them that draw iniquity with cords of vanity, and sin as it were with a cart rope.

Woe unto them that call evil good, and good evil; that put darkness for light, and light for darkness; that put bitter for sweet, and sweet for bitter!

Woe unto them that are wise in their own eyes, and prudent in their own sight!

Woe unto them that are mighty to drink wine, and men of strength to mingle strong drink:

Which justify the wicked for reward, and take away the righteousness of the righteous from him."

We read these words, and it seems to us that they have nothing to do with us.

We read in the Gospel, Matthew iii., 10: "And even now is the axe laid unto the root of the tree: every tree therefore that bringeth not forth good fruit is hewn down, and cast into the fire," and we are quite sure that the good tree bearing good fruit is we ourselves, and that those words are said, not to us, but to some other bad men.

We read the words of Isaiah vi., 10:

"Make the heart of this people fat, and make their ears heavy, and shut their eyes; lest they see with their eyes, and hear with their ears, and understand with their heart, and turn again, and be healed. Then said I, Lord, how long? And he answered, Until cities be waste without inhabitant, and houses without man, and the land become utterly waste."

We read, and are quite assured that this wonderful thing has not happened to us, but to some other people. For this very reason we do not see that this has happened to us, and is taking place with us. We do not hear, we do not see, and do not understand with our heart.

But why has it so happened?

CHAPTER XXVI

How can a man who considers himself to be,—we will not say a Christian or an educated and humane man,—but simply a man not entirely devoid of reason and of conscience,—how can he, I say, live in such a way, taking no part in the struggle of all mankind for life, only swallowing up the labour of others struggling for existence, and by his own claims increasing the labour of those who struggle and the number of those who perish in the struggle?

Such men abound in our so-called Christian and cultured world; and not only do they abound in our world but the very ideal of the men of our Christian, cultured world, is to get the largest amount of property,—that is, wealth,—which secures all comforts and idleness of life by freeing its possessors from the struggle for existence, and enabling them, as much as possible, to profit by the labour of those brothers of theirs who perish in that struggle.

How could men have fallen into such astounding error?

How could they have come to such a state that they can neither see nor hear nor understand with their heart what is so clear, obvious, and certain?

One need only think for a moment in order to be terrified at the way our lives contradict what we profess to believe, whether we be Christian or only humane educated people. Whether it be God or a law of nature that governs the world and men, good or bad, the position of men in this world, so long as we know it has always been such that naked men,—without wool on their bodies, without holes in which to take refuge, without food which they might find in the field like Robinson Crusoe on his island,—are put into a position of continual and incessant struggle with nature in order to cover their bodies by making clothes for themselves, to protect themselves by a roof over their heads, and to earn food in order twice or thrice a day to satisfy their hunger and that of their children and their parents.

Wherever and whenever and to whatever extent we observe the lives of men, whether in Europe, America, China, or Russia; whether we take into consideration all mankind or a small portion, whether in olden times in a nomad state, or in modern times with steam-engines, steam-ploughs, sewing-machines, and electric light,—we shall see one and the same thing going on,—that men, working constantly and incessantly, are not able to get clothes, shelter, and food for themselves, their little ones, and the old, and that the greatest number of men in olden times as well as now, perish slowly from want of the necessaries of life and from overwork.

Wherever we may live, if we draw a circle around us of a hundred thousand, or a thousand or ten, or even one mile's circumference, and look at the lives of those men who are inside our circle, we shall find half-starved children, old people male and female, pregnant women, sick and weak persons, working beyond their strength, who have neither food nor rest enough to support them, and who, for this reason, die before their time: we shall see others full-grown who are even being killed by dangerous and hurtful tasks.

Since the world has existed we find that with great efforts, sufferings, and privations men have been struggling for their common wants, and have not been able to overcome the difficulty.

Besides, we also know that every one of us, wherever and however he may live, *nolens volens*, is every day, and every hour of the day, absorbing for himself a part of the labour performed by mankind.

Wherever and however a man lives, the roof over his head did not grow of itself; the firewood in his stove did not get there of itself; the water did not come of itself either; and the baked bread does not fall down from the sky; his dinner, his clothes, and the covering for his feet, all this has been made for him, not only by men of past generations, long dead, but it is being done for him now by those men of whom hundreds and thousands are fainting away and dying in vain efforts to get for themselves and for their children sufficient shelter, food, and clothes,—means to save themselves and their children from suffering and a premature death.

All men are struggling with want. They are struggling so intensely that around them always their brethren, fathers, mothers, children, are perishing. Men in this world are like those on a dismantled or water-logged ship with a short allowance of food; all are put by God, or by nature, in such a position that they must husband their food and unceasingly war with want.

Each interruption in this work of every one of us, each absorption of the labour of others which is useless for the common welfare, is ruinous, alike for us and them.

How is it that the majority of educated people, without labouring, are quietly absorbing the labours of others which are necessary for their own lives, and are considering such an existence quite natural and reasonable?

If we are to free ourselves from the labour proper and natural to all and lay it on others, and yet not at the same time consider ourselves traitors and thieves, we can do so only by two suppositions,—first, that we (the men who take no part in common labour) are different beings from working-men and have a peculiar destiny to fulfil in society (like drone-bees, or queen-bees, which have a different function from the working-bees); or secondly, that the business which we (the men freed from the struggle for existence) are doing for other men is so useful for all that it undoubtedly compensates for that harm which we do to others in overburdening them.

In olden times men who lived by the labour of others asserted, first, that they belonged to a different race; and secondly, that they had from God a peculiar mission,—caring for the welfare of others; in other words, to govern and teach them: and therefore, they assured others, and partly believed themselves, that the business they did was more useful and more important for the people than those labours by which they profit. This justification was sufficient so long as the direct interference of God in human affairs, and the inequality of human races, was not doubted.

But with Christianity and that consciousness of the equality and unity of all men which proceeds from it, this justification could no longer be expressed in its previous form.

It was no longer possible to assert that men are born of different kind and quality and have a different destiny; and the old justification, though still held by some, has been little by little destroyed and has now almost entirely disappeared.

But though the justification disappeared, the fact itself,—of the freeing of some men from labour, and the appropriation by them of other men's labour, remained the same for those who had the power to enforce it. For this existing fact new excuses have constantly been invented, in order that without asserting the difference of human beings, men might be able with apparent justice to free themselves from personal labour.

A great many justifications have been invented. However strange it may seem, the main object of all that has been called science, and the ruling tendency of science, has been to seek out such excuses.

This has been the object of the theological sciences and of the science of law: this was the object of so-called philosophy, and this became lately the object of modern rationalistic science, however strange it appears to us, the contemporaries, who use this justification.

All the theological subtleties which aimed at proving that a certain church is the only true successor of Christ, and that, therefore, she alone has full and uncontrolled power over the souls and bodies of men, had in view this very object.

All the legal sciences,—those of state law, penal law, civil law, and international law,—have this sole aim.

The majority of philosophical theories, especially that of Hegel, which reigned over the minds of men for such a long time, and maintained the assertion that everything which exists is reasonable, and that the state is a necessary form of the development of human personality, had only this one object in view.

Comte's positive philosophy and its outcome, the doctrine that mankind is an organism; Darwin's doctrine of the struggle for existence, directing life and its conclusion, the theory of the diversity of human races, the anthropology now so popular, biology, and sociology,—all have the same aim. These sciences have become favourites, because they all serve for the justification of the existing fact of some men being able to free themselves from the human duty of labour, and to consume other men's labour.

All these theories, as is always the case, are worked out in the mysterious sanctums of augurs, and in vague, unintelligible expressions are spread abroad among the masses and adopted by them.

As in olden times the subtleties of theology, which justified violence in church and state, were the special property of priests; and among the masses of the people, the conclusions, taken by faith, and ready made for them, were circulated, that the power of kings, clergy and nobility was sacred: so afterwards, the philosophical and legal subtleties of so-called science became the property of the priests of science; and through the masses only the ready-made conclusion, accepted by faith,—that social order (the organization of society) must be such as it is, and cannot be otherwise,—was diffused.

So it is now. It is only in the sanctuaries of the modern sages that the laws of life and the development of organisms are analyzed. Whereas in the crowd, the ready-made conclusion, accepted on trust,—that division of labour is a law confirmed by science, and therefore it must be that some starve and toil and others eternally feast, and that this very ruin of some and feasting of others is the undoubted law of man's life, to which we must submit,—is circulated.

The current justification of their idleness by all so-called educated people, with their various activities, from the railway proprietor down to the author or artist, is this: We men who have freed ourselves from the common human duty of taking part in the struggle for existence, are furthering progress, and so we are of great use to all human society, of such use that we counterbalance all the harm we do the people by consuming their labour.

This reasoning seems to the men of our day to be not at all like the reasoning by which the former non-workers justified themselves; just as the reasoning of the Roman emperors and citizens, that but for them the civilized world would go to ruin, seemed to them to be of quite another order from that of the Egyptians and Persians; and so also an exactly similar kind of reasoning seemed in turn to the knights and clergy of the Middle Ages totally different from that of the Romans.

But it only *seems*. One need only reflect on the justification of our time in order to ascertain that there is nothing new in it. It is only a little differently dressed up, but it is the same because it is based on the same principle. Every justification of one man's consumption of the labour of others, while producing none himself, as with Pharaoh and his soothsayers, the emperors of Rome and those of the Middle Ages and their citizens, knights, priests, and clergy, always consists in these two assertions: First, we take the labour of the masses because we are different from others, people called by God to govern them and to teach them divine truths: Secondly, those who compose the masses cannot be judges of the measure of labour which we take from them for the good we do for them, because, as it has been said by the Pharisees, "This multitude which knoweth not the law are accursed" (John vii. 49).

The people do not understand what is for their good, and therefore they cannot be judges of the benefits done to them. The justification of our time, notwithstanding all apparent originality, consists in facts of the same fundamental assertions: First, we are a different people,—we are an educated people,—we further progress and civilization, and by this fact we procure for the masses a great advantage. Secondly, the uneducated crowd does not understand the advantages we procure for them, and therefore cannot be judges of them.

The fundamental assertions are the same. We free ourselves from labour, appropriate the labour of others, and by this increase the burden of our fellows; and then assert that in compensation for this we bring them a great advantage, of which they, owing to ignorance, cannot be judges.

Is it not, then, the same thing? The only difference lies in this: that formerly the claims on other men's labour were made by citizens, Roman priests, knights, and nobility, and now these claims are put forward by a caste who term themselves educated.

The lie is the same, because the men who justify themselves are in the same false position. The lie consists in the fact, that, before beginning to reason about the advantages conferred on the workers by people who have freed themselves from labour,—certain men, Pharaohs, priests, or we ourselves, educated people, assume this position first, and only afterwards manufacture a justification for it.

The very position universally serves as a basis for the justification. The difference of our justification from the ancient ones consists merely in the fact that it is more false and less well grounded. The old emperors and popes, if they themselves, and the people, believed in their divine calling, could easily explain why they were to control the labour of others: they asserted that they were appointed by God himself for this very thing, and from God they had a commandment to teach the people divine truths revealed to them, and to govern them.

But modern, educated men, who do not labour with their hands, and who acknowledge the equality of all men, cannot explain why they and their children (for education is only by money; that is, by power) should be those lucky persons called to an easy, idle life, out of those millions who by hundreds and thousands are perishing to make it possible for them to be educated. Their only justification consists in this, that, just as they are, instead of doing harm to the workers by freeing themselves from labour, and by swallowing up labour, they bring to the people some advantages, unintelligible to them, which compensate for all the evil they perpetrate.

CHAPTER XXVII

The theory by which men who have freed themselves from personal labour justify themselves, is, in its simplest and most exact form, this: "We men, having freed ourselves from work, and having by violence appropriated the labour of others, we find ourselves better able to benefit them." In other words, certain men, for doing the people a palpable and comprehensible harm,—utilizing their labour by violence, and thereby increasing the difficulty of their struggles with nature,—do to them an impalpable and incomprehensible good. This is a very strange proposition; but the men, both of former as well of modern times, who have lived on the labour of workmen, believe it, and calm their conscience by it.

Let us see in what way it is justified, in different classes of men who have freed themselves from labour in our own days.

"I serve men by my activity in church or state,—as king, minister, archbishop; I serve men by my trading or by industry; I serve men by my activity in the departments of science or art. By our activities we are all as necessary to the people as they are to us."

So say various men of to-day who have freed themselves from labour.

Let us consider *seriatim* the principles upon which they base the usefulness of their activity.

There are only two indications of the usefulness of any activity of one man for another: (1) an exterior indication,—the acknowledgement of the utility of the activity by those to whom it is applied; and (2) an interior indication,—the desire to be of use to others lying at the root of the activity of the one who is trying to be of use.

Statesmen (I include the Church dignitaries appointed by the government in the category of statesmen) are, it is said, of use to those whom they govern. The emperor, the king, the president of a republic, the prime minister, the minister of justice, the minister of war, the minister of public instruction, the bishop, and all under them who serve the state, all live free from the struggle of mankind for existence, having laid all the burden of this struggle on someone else, on the ground that their non-activity compensates for this.

Let us apply the first indication to those for whose welfare the activity of statesmen is bestowed. Do they, I ask, recognize the usefulness of this activity?

Yes, it is recognized. Most men consider statesmanship necessary to them. The majority recognize the usefulness of this activity in principle; but in all its manifestations known to us, in all *particular* cases known to us, the usefulness of each of the institutions and of each of the manifestations of this activity is not only denied by those for whose advantage it is performed, but they assert that it is even pernicious and hurtful. There is no state function or social activity which is not considered by many men to be hurtful: there is no institution which is not considered pernicious,—courts of justice, banks, local self-government, police, clergy. Every state activity, from the minister down to the policeman, from the bishop to the sexton, is considered by some men to be useful and by others to be pernicious. And this is the case not only in Russia but throughout the world; in France as well as in America.

The activity of the republican party is considered pernicious by the radical party, and *vice versa*: the activity of the radical party, if the power is in their hands, is considered bad by the republican and other parties. But not only is it a fact that the activity of statesmen is never considered by all men to be useful, this activity has, besides, this peculiarity, that it must always be carried out by violence, and that, to attain its end, murders, executions, prisons, taxes raised by force, and so on, became necessary.

It appears therefore that besides the fact that the usefulness of state activity is not recognized by all men, and is always denied by one portion of men, this usefulness has the peculiarity of vindicating itself always by violence.

Therefore the usefulness of state activity cannot be confirmed by the first indication,— i.e., the fact that it is recognized by those men for whom it is said to be performed.

Let us apply the second test. Let us ask statesmen themselves, from the Tsar down to the policeman, from the president to the secretary, from the patriarch to the sexton, begging for a sincere answer, whether, in occupying their respective positions they have in view the good which they wish to do for men or something else. In their desire to fill the situation of a Tsar, a president, a minister, a police-sergeant, a sexton, a teacher, are they moved by the desire of being useful to men or for their own personal advantage? And the answer of sincere men would be that their chief motive is their own personal advantage.

So it appears that one class of men, who live by the labour of some others who are perishing by these labours, compensate for this indubitable evil by an activity which is always considered by a great many men to be not only useless, but pernicious; which cannot be accepted voluntarily, but to which men must always be compelled, and the aim of which is not the benefit of others but the personal advantage of the men who perform it.

What is it, then, that confirms the theory that state activity is useful for humanity? Only the fact that the men who perform it firmly profess to believe it to be useful, and that it has been always in existence. But so some not only useless, but very pernicious institutions, like slavery, prostitution, and wars, have always been in existence.

Business people (merchants, manufacturers, railway proprietors, bankers, land-owners) believe that they do a good which compensates for the harm undoubtedly done by them. On what grounds do they believe this? To the question, By whom is the usefulness of their activity recognized? men in church and in state are able to point to the thousands and millions of working-people who in principle recognize the usefulness of state and church activity. But to whom will bankers, distillers, manufacturers of velvet, of bronzes, of looking-glasses, to say nothing of guns,—to whom will they point when we ask them, Is their usefulness recognized by public opinion?

If men can be found who recognize the usefulness of manufacturing chintzes, rails, beer, and such like things, there will be found also a still greater number of men who consider the manufacture of these articles pernicious.

As for the merchants whose activity is confined to prices, and land-owners, nobody would even attempt to justify them.

Besides, this activity is always associated with harm to working-people, and with violence, which, if less direct than that of the state, is yet just as cruel in its consequences. For the activities displayed in industry and in trade are entirely based on taking advantage of the wants of working-people in every form in order to compel them to hard and hated labour; to buying cheap, and to selling necessaries at the highest possible price and to raising the interest on money. From whatever point we consider this activity we can see that the usefulness of business-men is not recognised by those for whom it is expended, neither generally nor in particular cases; and by the majority their activity is considered to be directly pernicious.

If we were to apply the second test and to ask, What is the chief motive of the activity of business-men? we should receive a still more determinate answer than that on the activity of statesmen. If a statesman says that besides a personal advantage he has in view the common benefit, we cannot help believing him, and each of us knows such men. But a business-man, from the very nature of his occupations cannot have in view a common advantage, and would be ridiculous in the sight of his fellows if he were in his business aiming at something besides increasing his wealth and keeping it.

And, therefore, working-people do not consider the activity of business-men of any advantage to them. Their activity is associated with violence; and its object is not their good but always and only personal advantage; and yet, strange to say, these business-men are so assured of their own usefulness that they boldly, for the sake of their imaginary good, do an undoubted, obvious harm to workmen by extricating themselves from labour, and consuming the produce of the working-classes.

Scientists and artists have also freed themselves from labour by putting it on others, and live with a quiet conscience believing that they bring sufficient advantages to other men to compensate for it. On what is this assurance based? Let us ask them as we have done statesmen and business-men. Is the utility of the arts and sciences recognized by all, or even by the majority, of working-people?

We shall receive a very sad answer. The activity of men in the State Church and government offices is recognized to be useful in theory by almost all, and in application by the majority of those for whom it is performed. The activity of business-men is recognized only by those who are engaged in it or who desire to practise it. Those who bear on their shoulders all the labour of life and who feed and clothe the scientists and artists cannot recognize the usefulness of the activity of these men because they cannot even form an idea about an activity which always appears to workmen useless and even depraving.

Thus, without any exception, working-people think the same about universities, libraries, conservatories, picture and statue galleries, and theatres, which are built at their expense.

A workman considers this activity so decidedly pernicious that he does not send his children to be taught; and in order to compel people to accept this activity it has everywhere been found necessary to introduce a law compelling parents to send the children to school.

A workman always looks at this activity with ill-will, and only ceases to look at it so when he ceases to be a workman, and through gain and so-called education passes out of the class of working-people into the class of men who live on the neck of others.

Notwithstanding the fact that the usefulness of the activity of scientists and artists is not recognized and even cannot be recognized by any workman, these men are, all the same, compelled to make sacrifices for such an activity.

A statesman simply sends another to the guillotine or to prison; a business-man, utilizing the labour of someone else, takes from him his last resource, leaving him the alternative of starvation or labour destructive to his health and life: but a man of science or of art seemingly compels nobody to do anything; he merely offers the good he has done to those who are willing to take it; but, to be able to make his productions undesirable to the working-people, he takes away from them by violence, through the statesmen, a great part of their labour for the building and keeping open of academies, universities, colleges, schools, museums, libraries, conservatories, and for the wages for himself and his fellows.

But if we were to ask the scientists and artists the object which they are pursuing in their activity, we should receive the most astonishing replies.

A statesman would answer that his aim was the common welfare; and in his answer, there would be an admixture of truth confirmed by public opinion.

In the answer of the business-man, there would be less probability; but we could admit even this also.

But the answer of the scientists and artists strikes one at once by its want of proof and by its effrontery. Such men say, without bringing any proofs (just as priests used to do in olden times) that their activity is the most important of all, and that without it mankind would go to ruin. They assert that it is so, notwithstanding the fact that nobody except themselves either understands or acknowledges their activity, and notwithstanding the fact that, according to their own definition, true science and true art should not have a utilitarian aim.

These men are occupied with the matter they like, without troubling themselves what advantage will come out of it to men; and they are always assured that they are doing the most important and the most necessary thing for all mankind.

So that while a sincere statesman, acknowledging that the chief motive of his activity is a personal one, tries to be as useful as possible to the working-people; while a business-man, acknowledging the egotism of his activity, tries to give it an appearance of being one of universal utility,—men of science and art do not consider it necessary even to seem to shelter themselves under a pretence of usefulness, they deny even the object of usefulness, so sure are they, not only of the usefulness but even of the sacredness of their own business.

So it turns out that the third class of men who have freed themselves from labour and laid it on others, are occupied with things which are totally incomprehensible to the working-people, and which these people consider trifles and often very pernicious trifles; and are occupied with these things without any consideration of their usefulness but merely for the gratification of their own pleasure: it turns out that these men are, from some reason or other, quite assured that their activity will always produce that without which the work-people would never be able to exist.

Men have freed themselves from labouring for their living and have thrown the work upon others who perish under it: they utilize this labour and assert that their occupations, which are incomprehensible to all other men, and which are not directed to useful aims, compensate for all the evil they are doing to men by freeing themselves from the trouble of earning their livelihood and by swallowing up the labour of others.

The statesman, to compensate for the undoubted and obvious evil which he does to man by freeing himself from the struggle with nature and by appropriating the labour of others, does men another obvious and undoubted harm by countenancing all sorts of violence.

The business-man, to compensate for the undoubted and obvious harm which he does to men by using up their labour, tries to earn for himself as much wealth as possible; that is, as much of other men's labour as possible.

The man of science and art, in compensating for the same undoubted and obvious harm which he does to working-people, is occupied with matters to which he feels attracted and which are quite incomprehensible to work-people, and which, according to his own assertion, in order to be true, ought not to aim at usefulness.

Therefore, all these men are quite sure that their right of utilizing other men's labour is secure. Yet it seems obvious that all those men who have freed themselves from the labour of earning their livelihood have no justification for doing so.

But, strange to say, these men firmly believe in their own righteousness, and live as they do with an easy conscience.

There must be some plausible ground, some false belief, at the bottom of such a profound error.

CHAPTER XXVIII

In reality, the position in which men who live by other men's labour are placed, is based not only on a certain belief but on an entire doctrine; and not only on one doctrine but on three, which have grown one upon another during centuries and are now fused together into an awful deceit,—or humbug as the English call it,—which hides from men their unrighteousness.

The oldest of these, which justifies the treason of men against the fundamental duty of labour to earn their own living, was the Church-Christian doctrine, which asserts that men by the will of God differ one from another as the sun differs from the moon and the stars, and as one star differs from another. Some men God has ordained to have dominion over all, others to have power over many, others, still, over a few, and the remainder are ordained by God to obey.

This doctrine, though already shaken to its foundations, still continues to influence some men, so that many who do not accept it, who often even ignore the existence of it, are, nevertheless, guided by it.

The second is what I cannot help terming the State-philosophical doctrine. According to this, as fully developed by Hegel, everything that exists is reasonable, and the established order of life is constant, and is sustained not merely by men, but as the only possible form of the manifestation of the spirit, or, generally, of the life of mankind.

This doctrine, too, is no longer accepted by the men who direct social opinion, and it holds its position only by the power of inertia.

The last doctrine, which is now ruling the minds of men and on which is based the justification of leading statesmen, men of business, and science and art, is a scientific one, not in the evident sense of the word (meaning knowledge generally), but in the sense of a knowledge peculiar in form as well as in matter, termed *Science*. On this new doctrine, the justification of man's idleness and the hiding from him his treason against his calling, is particularly based.

This doctrine appeared in Europe contemporaneously with a large class of rich and idle people who served neither the church nor the state and who were in want of a justification of their position.

Not very long ago, before the French revolution in Europe, all non-working people, in order to have a right to utilize other men's labour, were obliged to have some definite occupation,—to serve in the church, the state, or the army.

The men who served the government, "governed the people"; those who served the church, "taught the people divine truths"; and those who served the army, "protected the people."

Only these three classes of men—the clergy, the statesmen, and the military men—claimed for themselves the right of utilizing labour, and they could always point out their services to the people: the remaining rich men who had not this justification, were despised, and, feeling their own want of right, were ashamed of their wealth and their idleness. But as time went on, this class of rich people, who belonged neither to the clergy, to the government, nor to the army, owing to the vices of these other three classes, increased in number and became a powerful party. They were in want of a justification of their position. And one was invented for them. A century had not elapsed before the men who served neither the State nor the Church and took no part whatever in their affairs, received the same right to live on labour as the former classes; and they not only left off being ashamed of their wealth and idleness but began to consider their position quite justified. And the number of such men has increased, and is still increasing in our days.

The most wonderful of all is this, that these men whose claims to be freed from labour were unrecognized not long ago, now consider themselves alone to be fully right and are attacking the former three classes,—the servants of the Church, State, and Army,—alleging their exemption from labour to be unjust and often even considering their activity directly pernicious. What is still more wonderful is this, that the former servants of Church, State, and Army, do not now lean on the divinity of their calling, nor even on the philosophy which considers the state necessary for individual development, but setting aside these supports which have so long maintained them, they are now seeking the same supports on which the new reigning class of men, who have found a novel justification, stand, and at the head of which are the men of Science and Art.

If a statesman now sometimes, appealing to old memories, justifies his position by the fact that he was set in it by God, or by the fact that the state is a form of the development of personality, he does it because he is behind the age, and he feels that nobody believes him.

In order to justify himself effectually, he ought to find now neither theological nor philosophical but new and scientific supports.

It is necessary to point to the principle of nationalities, or to that of the development of an organism; and to gain over the ruling class, as in the Middle Ages it was necessary to gain over the clergy; and as at the end of the last century, it was necessary to obtain the sanction of philosophers, as seen in the case of Frederick the Great and Catherine of Russia. If now a rich man, after the old fashion, says sometimes that it is God's providence which makes him rich, or if he points to the importance of a nobility for the welfare of a state, he does it because he is behind the times.

In order to justify himself completely he must point to the way he furthers progress by improving the modes of production, by lowering the prices of consumption, by establishing intercourse between nations. A rich man must think and speak in scientific language, and, like the clergy formerly, he must offer sacrifices to the ruling class: he must publish magazines and books, provide himself with a picture-gallery, a musical society, a kindergarten or technical school. The ruling class is the class of learned men and artists of a definite character. They possess the complete justification for having freed themselves from labour; and on this justification (as in former times on the theological justification, and afterwards on the philosophical one) everything is based: and it is these men who now give the diploma of exemption to other classes.

The class of men who now feel completely justified in freeing themselves from labour, is that of men of science, and particularly of experimental, positive, critical, evolutional science, and of artists who develop their ideas according to the same tendency.

If a learned man or an artist of the old style speaks nowadays about prophecy, revelation, or the manifestation of the spirit, he does so because he is behind the age, and he will not succeed in justifying himself: to stand firm he must try to associate his activity with experimental, positive, critical science, and he must make this science the fundamental principle of his activity. Only then will the science or the art with which he is occupied appear true, and he will stand on firm ground, and then there will be no doubt as to his usefulness to mankind. The justification of all who have freed themselves from labour is now based upon this experimental, critical, positive science.

The theological and philosophical explanations have had their day: now they timidly and bashfully introduce themselves to notice and try to humour their scientific usurper, who, however, boldly knocks down and destroys the remnants of the past, everywhere taking its place, and, assured of its own firmness, lifts aloft its head.

The theological justification maintained that men are predestined,—some to govern, others to obey; some to live sumptuously, others to labour: and therefore those who believed in the revelation of God could not doubt the lawfulness of the position of those men, who, by the will of God, are called to govern and to be rich.

The state-philosophical justification used to say, "The state with all its institutions and differences of classes according to rights and possessions, is that historical form which is necessary for the right manifestation of the spirit in mankind; and therefore the situation which everyone occupies in state and in society according to his rights and to his possessions must be such as to ensure the sound life of mankind."

The scientific theory says, "All this is nonsense and superstition: the one is the fruit of the theological period of thought, and the other of the metaphysical period. To study the laws of the life of human societies, there is only one sure method,—that of a positive, experimental, critical science. It is only sociology, based on biology, in its turn based on all the other positive sciences, which is able to give us new laws for the life of mankind. Mankind, or human societies, are organisms either already perfect, or in a state of development subject to the laws of the evolution of organisms. One of the first of these laws is the division of labour among the portions of the organs. If some men govern and others obey, some live in opulence and others in want, then this is so, neither according to the will of God nor because the state is the form of the manifestation of personality, but because in societies as in organisms a division of labour takes place which is necessary for the life of the whole. Some men perform in societies the muscular part of labour, and others, the mental."

On this doctrine is built the ruling excuse of the age.

CHAPTER XXIX

Christ teaches men in a new way, and this teaching is written down in the Gospels.

It is first persecuted, and not accepted. Then the fables of the fall of man, and of the first angel, are invented, and these fables are believed to be the teaching of Christ. The fables are absurd, they have no foundation whatever, but by virtue of them men are led to believe that they may continue to live in an evil way, and none the less consider themselves as saved by Christ. This conclusion is so agreeable to the mass of weak men who have no affection for moral effort, that the system is eagerly accepted, not only as true, but even as the Divine truth as revealed by God himself. And the invention becomes the groundwork on which for centuries theologians build their theories.

Then by degrees these learned men diverge by various channels into special systems of their own, and finally endeavour to overthrow each other's theories. They begin to feel there is something amiss, and cease to understand what they themselves are talking about. But the crowd still requires them to expound its favourite instruction; and thus the theologians, pretending both to understand and believe what they are saying, continue to dispense it.

In process of time, however, the conclusions drawn from theological conceptions cease to be necessary to the masses, who, then, peeping into the very sanctuaries of their augurs, discover them to be utterly void of those glorious and indubitable truths which the mysteries of theology had seemed to be, and see instead that there is nothing there but crude deception, and they marvel at their own blindness.

The same happened to philosophy, not in the sense of the wisdom of men like Confucius or Epictetus, but with professional philosophy which humoured the instincts of the crowd of rich and idle people. Not long ago a moral philosophy was in fashion in the learned world, according to which it appeared that everything that is, is reasonable; that there is neither good nor evil; that man has not to struggle with evil, but has merely to manifest the spirit of the age, some in military service, some in courts of justice, and some on the violin.

Many and various were the expressions of human wisdom known to the men of the nineteenth century,—of Rousseau, Pascal, Lessing, and Spinoza; and all the wisdom of antiquity was expounded, but none of its systems laid hold of the crowd. We cannot say that Hegel's success was due to the harmony of his theory. We had no less harmonious theories from Descartes, Leibnitz, Fichte, and Schopenhauer.

There was only one reason for the fact that this doctrine became for a short time the belief of the civilized world, the same reason that caused the success of the theory of the fall and redemption of man; to wit, that the deductions of this philosophical theory humoured the weak side of men's nature. It said, "All is reasonable, all is good; nobody is to blame for any thing."

As at first with the church upon theological foundations, so also, with the philosophy of Hegel for a base, a Babel's tower was built (some who are behind the age are still sitting upon it); and here again was a confusion of tongues, men feeling that they themselves did not know of what they were talking, but were trying to conceal their ignorance and keep up their prestige before the crowd; and here again the masses found confirmation of their accepted teachings, and believed that whatever might seem to them bewildering and contradictory is as clear as day-light on philosophic altitudes. In the same way, the time came when this doctrine wore out and a new one replaced it. It had become useless, and the crowd peeped into the mysterious temples of the teachers, and saw there was nothing there—nor ever had been, but obscure and unmeaning words. I have seen this in my own day.

When I began life, Hegelianism was the order of the day; it was in the very air you breathed; it found its expression in newspapers and magazines, in lectures on history and on law, in novels, in tracts, in art, in sermons, in conversation. A man who did not know Hegel had no right to open his mouth; those who desired to learn the truth were studying Hegel,—every thing pointed to him; and lo! forty years have elapsed and nothing is left of him; there is no remembrance of him; all is as though he had never existed. And the most remarkable of all is, that just as false Christianity, so also Hegelianism has fallen, not because someone refuted or overthrew it; no, it is now as it was before, but both have only become no longer necessary for the learned, educated world.

If at the present time we speak to any man of modern culture about the fall of the angel, of Adam, about atonement, he does not argue or deny;—he simply asks, amazed, "What angel? Adam? What for? What atonement? What is all this to me?"

So also with Hegelianism. No one of our day will argue its theses. He will only inquire, "What Spirit?" "Where did it come from?" "With what purpose?" "What good will it do me?" Not very long ago the sages of Hegelianism were solemnly teaching the crowd; and the crowd, understanding nothing, blindly believed all, finding the confirmation of what suited them, and thinking that what seemed to them to be not quite clear or even contradictory, was clearer than day on the heights of philosophy: but time went on, the theory was worn out, a new one appeared in its place, the former one was no longer demanded, and again the crowd looked into the mysterious temples of the augurs and saw there was nothing there, and that nothing had ever been there but words, very dark and meaningless.

This happened within my memory. These things happened, we are told, because they were ravings of the theological and metaphysical period, but now we have a critical, positive science which will not deceive us, because it is based upon induction and experience; now our knowledge is no longer uncertain as it formerly was, and it is only by following it that one can find the answer to all the questions of life.

But this is exactly what was said by the old teachers, and they certainly were no fools, and we know that among them were men of immense intellect; and within my memory the disciples of Hegel said exactly the same thing, with no less assurance and no less acknowledgment on the side of the crowd of so-called educated people. And such men as our Herzen, Stankievich, Bylinsky, were no fools either. But why, then, has this wonderful thing happened, that clever men preached with the greatest assurance and the crowd accepted with veneration, only groundless and meaningless doctrines? The reason is only that these doctrines justified men in their bad mode of living.

A very commonplace English writer, whose books are now almost forgotten and recognized as the emptiest of all empty ones, wrote a tract upon population, in which he invented an imaginary law that the means of living do not increase with the increase of population. This sham law the author dressed out with the formulæ of mathematics which have no foundation whatever, and published it. Judged by the lightness of mind and the want of talent displayed in this treatise we might have supposed that it would have passed unnoticed and been forgotten as all other writings of the same author have been; but it turned out quite differently. The author who wrote it became at once a scientific authority, and has maintained this position for nearly half a century. Malthus! The Malthusian theory,—the law of the increase of population in geometrical progression, and the increase of means of living in arithmetical progression, and the natural and prudent means of restraining the increase of population,—all these became scientific, undoubted truths which have never been verified, but, accepted as axioms, have served for further deductions.

Thus learned and educated men were deceived; whereas in the crowd of idle men there was a blind and religious trust in the great laws discovered by Malthus. How did this happen? These statements seem to be scientific deductions which have nothing in common with the instincts of the crowd.

But they are only sacred to those who believe science to be something self-existent and infallible, like the Church, and not merely the thoughts of weak men liable to mistakes, who only for importance' sake call their own thoughts and words by a pompous word, *science*. It was only necessary to draw practical conclusions from the Malthusian theory in order to see that it was quite a human one with very determinate aims.

The deductions which were directly drawn from this theory were the following: The miserable condition of working-people does not come from the cruelty, egotism, and unreasonableness of rich and powerful men, but it exists according to an unchangeable law which does not depend upon man, and, if anybody is to blame, it is the starving working-people themselves: why do these fools come into the world when they know that they will not have enough to eat? and therefore the wealthy and powerful classes are not at all to blame for any thing, and they may quietly continue to live as they have done.

This conclusion, being pleasant to the crowd of idle men, induced the learned dons to overlook the incorrectness and total arbitrariness of the deductions; and the crowd of educated, i.e., idle people, instinctively guessing to what these deductions led, greeted the theory with delight, set upon it the seal of truth, and cherished it during half a century. The reason for all this was, that these doctrines justified men in their bad mode of life.

Is not the same cause at the bottom of the self-assurance of men of the new positive, critical, experimental science, and of the reverent regard of the crowd to what they preach? At first it seems strange that the theory of evolution (like the theory of atonement in theology, it serves for the majority of men as a popular expression of the new teaching) should justify men in their false lives, and it would seem that the scientific theory has only to do with facts, and does nothing but observe facts. But it only seems so.

It had been so with theological teaching; theology seemed to be occupied only with doctrines and to have nothing to do with the lives of men. It had been so with philosophy, which also seemed to be occupied only with facts.

It had been so with the teaching of Hegel on a large scale, and with the theory of Malthus on a small one. Hegelianism seemed to be occupied merely with its logical constructions and to have nothing to do with the lives of men; and the theory of Malthus seemed to be occupied exclusively with statistics.

But it only seemed so.

Modern science also claims to be occupied exclusively with facts: it studies facts.

But what facts? Why some facts and not others?

The disciples of the modern science are very fond of saying with a solemn assurance, "We study facts alone," imagining that these words have some meaning.

To study facts alone is quite impossible, because the number of facts which may be objects of our study, are, in the strict sense of the word, countless.

Before beginning to study facts, one must have some theory according to which the facts are studied; that is, determining which shall be selected from the countless number of facts. And this theory indeed exists and is even very definitely expressed, though many of the agents of modern science ignore it; that is, do not want to know it, or really do not know it;—sometimes pretend not to know it.

Thus matters stood before with all most important beliefs.

The basis of each is always given in theory; and so-called learned men seek only further deductions from the various bases given to them, though sometimes they ignore even these.

But a fundamental theory must always be present, and so it is also now. Modern science selects its facts on the ground of a determinate theory, which sometimes it knows, sometimes does not wish to know, sometimes really does not know; but which exists. The theory is this: Mankind is an undying organism, having each his special calling for the service of the whole. As the cells, growing into an organism, divide among themselves the labour of the struggle for existence of the whole organism, increase one capacity, and diminish another, and all together form an organ in order better to satisfy the wants of the whole organism; and as among social animals,—ants and bees,—the individuals divide the labour among themselves (queen-bees lay eggs, drone-bees fecundate, working-bees labour for the life of the whole),—so also in mankind and in human societies there take place the same differentiation and integration of the parts. And therefore, in order to find the law of man's life, we must study the laws of the lives and development of organisms. And in these we find the following laws: That each phenomenon is followed by more than one consequence. The failure of uniformity. The law of uniformity and diversity; and so on.

All this seems to be very innocent, but we need only draw deductions from these observations of facts in order to see at once to what they are tending. These facts lead to one thing,—the acknowledgement of humanity or human society as an organism, and hence to the acknowledgment of the division of activities in human society as organic, that is necessary; and as there exist in human societies many cruelties and vices, therefore these phenomena must not be considered as cruelties and vices, but must be accepted as inevitable facts confirming a general law—i.e., that of "division of labour." Moral philosophy used also to justify every cruelty and wickedness; but there it became philosophical, and therefore incorrect. According to science, however, the same thing turns out to be scientific, and therefore unquestionable.

How can we help accepting such a fine theory! We need only look at human society merely as something to be observed, and we may quietly devour the labour of perishing men, calming ourselves with the idea that our activity as a dancing-master, a lawyer, a doctor, a philosopher, an actor, an investigator of the theory of mediumism and of forms of atoms, and so on, is a functional activity of the organism of mankind and therefore there can be no question whether it is just that I should continue to live doing only what is pleasant, just as there can be no question whether the division of labour between a mental and a muscular cell is fair or not. How can we help accepting such a nice theory which enables us afterwards to put our consciences into our pockets forever, and live a completely unbridled, animal life, feeling under our feet a firm, scientific support? And it is upon this new belief that the justification of idleness and the cruelty of men is built.

CHAPTER XXX

This doctrine had its commencement about half a century ago. Its chief founder was the French philosopher Comte. Comte, being a lover of systematic theory, and at the same time a man of religious tendency, was impressed by the then new physiological researches of Bichat; and he conceived the old idea, expressed in bygone days by Menenius Agrippa, that human societies, indeed all human-kind, may be regarded as one whole, An Organism, and men—as live particles of separate organs, each having his definite destination to fulfil in the service of the whole organism.

Comte was so fascinated by this idea that he founded his philosophical theory on it; and this theory so captivated him that he quite forgot that his point of departure was no more than a pretty comparison, suitable enough in a fable, but in no way justifiable as the foundation of a science. As it often happens, he took his pet hypothesis for an axiom, and so imagined that his whole theory was based upon the most firm and positive foundations.

According to his theory it appeared that, as mankind is an organism, therefore the knowledge of what man is and what his relation to the world ought to be, is only possible through the knowledge of the properties of this organism. And to be able to learn these properties man is fitted to make observations upon other lower organisms and to draw deductions from their lives.

Therefore, first, the true and exclusive method of science, according to Comte, is the inductive one, and science is only science when it has experiment for its basis. Secondly, the final aim and the summit of science becomes the new science concerning the imaginary organism of Mankind, or the organic being,—Mankind. This new hypothetic science is Sociology. From this view of science it generally turns out that all former knowledge was false, and that the whole history of mankind, in the sense of its self-consciousness, divides itself into three, or rather two, periods. First, the theological and metaphysical period, from the beginning of the world to Comte. And, secondly, the modern period of true science, positive science, beginning with Comte.

All this was very well, but there was one mistake in it, which was this: that all this edifice was built on the sand, on an arbitrary (and incorrect) assertion that mankind, collectively considered, was an organism.

This assertion is arbitrary because, if we are to acknowledge the existence of mankind as an organism, which is beyond observation, we might as well acknowledge the existence of the triple God and similar theological propositions.

It was incorrect, because to the idea of mankind, that is, of men, the definition of an organism was added, whereas man lacks the essential characteristics of an organism,—a centre of sensation or consciousness. We call an elephant, as well as a bacterium, organisms, only because we suppose by analogy in these beings that there is unification of sensations, or consciousness. But human societies and mankind lack this essential; and therefore, however many other general character-signs we may find in mankind and in an organism,—without this, the assertion that man is an organism is incorrect.

But notwithstanding the arbitrariness and incorrectness of the fundamental proposition of Positive Philosophy, it was accepted by the so-called "Educated World" with great sympathy, because of that great fact, important for the crowd, that it afforded a justification of the existing order of things by recognizing the lawfulness of the existing division of labour; that is, of violence in mankind. It is remarkable in this respect that from the writings of Comte, composed of two parts,—a Positive Philosophy and a Positive Politics,—only the first part was accepted on new experimental principles by the learned world, that which justified the existing evil in human society. The second part, treating of the moral, altruistic duties, following from this recognition of mankind as an organism, was considered not only unimportant but even unscientific.

Here the same thing was repeated which occurred with the two parts of Kant's writings. The "Critique of Pure Reason," was accepted by science; but the "Critique of Practical Reason," that part which contains the essence of moral doctrine, was rejected. In the teaching of Comte, that was recognized to be scientific which humoured the reigning evil.

But the Positive Philosophy accepted by the crowd, based on an arbitrary and incorrect supposition, was by itself too ill-grounded, and therefore too unsteady, and could not be sustained by itself.

And now, among the idle play of ideas of so-called "Men of Science," there has appeared a similarly arbitrary and incorrect assertion, not at all new, to the effect that all living beings (that is, organisms), proceed one from another; not only one organism from another, but one organism from many; that during a very long period, a million of years, for instance, not only may a fish and a duck have proceeded from one and the same forefather, but also one organism might have proceeded from many separate organisms; so, for instance, out of a swarm of bees a single animal may proceed. This arbitrary and incorrect assertion was accepted by the learned world with still greater sympathy.

The assertion was arbitrary, because no one has ever seen how one kind of organism is made from others; and therefore the hypothesis about the Origin of Species will always remain a mere supposition and never become an experimental fact.

The hypothesis was incorrect, because the solution of the problem of the Origin of Species by the theory of the laws of inheritance and accommodation during an infinitely long period, is not a solution of the problem at all, but the mere reiteration of the question in another form.

According to the solution of this problem by Moses (to oppose which is the object of Comte's theory), it appeared that the variety of the species of living beings proceeded from the will of God and his infinite omnipotence. According to the Theory of Evolution, it appears that the variety of species of living beings proceeded from themselves in consequence of the infinite variety of conditions of inheritance and environment in an infinite period of time.

The Theory of Evolution, speaking plainly, asserts only that (by chance) in an infinite period of time, anything you like may proceed from anything else you choose.

This is no answer to the question; it is simply the same question put differently: instead of Will is put Chance, and the co-efficient of the Infinite is transferred from Omnipotence to Time.

But this new assertion, enforced by Darwin's followers in an arbitrary and inaccurate spirit, maintained the first assertion of Comte, and therefore it became the Revelation for our time, and the foundation of all sciences, even that of the history of philosophy and religion; and besides, according to the *naïve* confession of Darwin himself, the idea was awakened in him by the law of Malthus; and therefore he pointed to the "Struggle for Existence" not only of men but of all living beings, as a fundamental law of every living thing, and this was exactly what was wanted by the crowd of idle people for their own justification.

Two unstable theories which could not stand on their own feet supported each other, and so received a show of stability. Both the theories bore in them a sense, precious to the crowd, that men are not to be blamed for the existing evil in human societies, that the existing order is what should be; and thus the new theory was accepted by the crowd in the sense wanted by them, with full confidence and unprecedented enthusiasm.

Thus the new scientific doctrine was founded upon two arbitrary and incorrect propositions, accepted in the same way that dogmas of faith are accepted. Both in matter and form this new doctrine is remarkably like the Church-Christian one. In matter, the similarity lies in the fact that in both doctrines alike a fantastical meaning is attached to really existing things, and this artificial meaning is taken as the object of our research.

In the Church-Christian doctrine, to Christ who did really exist, is attributed the fantastic conception of being God Himself, screened. In the Positive doctrine, to the really existing fact of live men is attributed the fantastical attributes of an organism.

In form, the similarity of these two doctrines is remarkable, since, in both cases, a theory emanating from one class of men is accepted as the only and infallible truth. In the Church-Christian doctrine, the Church's way of understanding God's revelation to men is regarded as the sacred and only true one. In the doctrine of Positivism, certain men's way of understanding science is regarded as absolutely correct and true.

As the Church-Christians regard the foundation of their church as the only origin of true knowledge of God, and only out of a kind of courtesy admit that former believers may also be regarded as having formed a church; so in precisely the same manner does Positive science, according to its own statement, place its origin in Comte: and its representatives, also only out of courtesy, admit the existence of previous science, and that only as regarding certain thinkers, as, for instance, Aristotle. Both the Church and Positive science altogether exclude the ideas of all the rest of mankind, and regard all knowledge outside their own as *erroneous*. The similarity persists. Just as to the support of the first advental theological dogmas of the Trinity and of the divinity of Christ comes the old—but newly-interpreted—dogmas of man's fall and of his redemption by the death of Christ, and out of these dogmas is developed popular Church teaching: so in our time, the old dogma of Evolution comes in with new importance to help the fundamental dogma of Comte concerning the organism of mankind; and from these two elements the popular scientific doctrine has been formed. As in one teaching, so in the other: the new dogma is necessary for the support of the old one, and becomes comprehensible only in connection with it. If to a believer in the Divinity of Christ, it is not clearly comprehensible why God should come down to earth, the doctrine of atonement explains it. If it is not quite clear to a believer in the Organism of Mankind why a collection of individuals may be counted as an organism, the dogma of Evolution is charged with the explanation. This dogma is needed to reconcile the contradictions and certainties of the first: mankind is an organism, and we see that it does not contain the chief characteristic of an organism; how must we account for it?

Here the dogma of evolution comes in, and explains, Mankind is an organism in a state of development. If you accept this, you may then consider mankind as such.

As to any man free from superstitions about the trinity and the Divinity of Christ, it is impossible even to understand the force and the meaning of the teaching of atonement, which meaning comes only through the acknowledgment of Christ as God Himself, so a man who is free from the Positive superstition cannot even understand wherein lies the interest of the theory of the Origin of Species and of Evolution; and this interest is explained only when we learn the fundamental dogma, that "Mankind is an Organism." And as the subtleties of theology are only intelligible to those who believe in its fundamental dogmas, so also the subtleties of sociology, which now occupy the minds of all adherents of this recent and profound science, are intelligible only to believers. The doctrine of atonement is necessary to reconcile the contradiction between the first dogma and facts. God descended on earth to save men. But men are not saved. How then explain this? The dogma of atonement asserts "He saved those, who believed in atonement. If you believe in atonement, you are saved."

The similarity between these two doctrines holds good yet further. Being founded on dogmas accepted by faith, these doctrines neither question nor analyze their own principles, which, on the other hand, are used as starting-points for the most extraordinary theories. The preachers of these call themselves, in Theology, sanctified; in Positive knowledge, scientific; in both cases, infallible. And at the same time, they conceive the most peremptory, incredible, and unfounded assertions, which they give forth with the greatest pomp and seriousness, and which are with equal pomp and seriousness contradicted in all their details by others who do not agree, and yet who equally recognize the fundamental dogmas.

The Basil the Great of scientific doctrine, Herbert Spencer, in one of his first writings expresses these doctrines thus: Societies and organisms, says he, are alike in the following points: First, in that, being conceived as small aggregates, they imperceptibly grow in mass, so that some of them become ten thousand times bigger than their originals.

Secondly, in that, while in the beginning they have such simple structure that they may almost be considered structureless, in their growth they develop an ever-increasing complexity of structure.

Thirdly, in that, though in their early undeveloped period there does not exist among them any dependence of particles upon one another, these particles by and by acquire a mutual dependence, which at last becomes so strong that the activity and the life of each part is possible only with the activity and the lives of all others.

Fourthly, in this, that the life and the development of society is more independent and longer than the life and the development of every unit which goes to form it, and which is separately born and growing and acting and multiplying and dying while the political body formed of such continues to live one generation after another, developing in mass, in perfection of structure, and in functional activity.

Then follow the points of difference between organisms and societies, and it is demonstrated that these differences are only seeming ones, and that organisms and societies are quite similar.

To an impartial man the question at once arises, What are you speaking about, then? Why is mankind an organism or something similar? You say that societies are similar to organisms according to these four points; but even this comparison is incorrect. You take only a few characteristics of an organism, and you then apply them to human societies. You produce four points of similarity, then you take the points of difference which you say are only seemingly so, and you conclude that human societies may be considered as organisms. But this is nothing else than an idle play of dialectics. On this ground we may consider as an organism everything we choose. I take the first thing which comes to my mind,—a forest, as it is planted in a field and grows up: first beginning as a small aggregate and imperceptibly increasing in mass. Secondly, "In the beginning the structure of an organism is simple, then the complexity increases," and so on. This is the case with the forest: at first there are only birch-trees, then hazel, and so on; first all the trees grow straight, and afterwards they interlace their branches. Thirdly, "The dependence of the parts increases so that the life of each part depends upon the lives and activities of all the others": it is exactly the same with the forest; the nut-tree keeps the trunks warm (if you hew it down, the other trees will be frozen in winter), the underwood keeps off wind, the seed-trees continue the species, the tall and leafy ones give shadow, and the life of each tree depends upon that of the rest. Fourthly, "Separate parts may die, but the whole organism continues to live." Separate trees perish, but the forest continues in life and growth.

The same holds good with the example so often brought by the defenders of the scientific doctrine. Cut off an arm,—the arm will die: we may say remove a tree from the shadow and the ground of a forest, it will die.

Another remarkable similarity between this scientific doctrine and the Church-Christian one,—and any other theory founded upon propositions which are accepted through faith,—lies in their mutual capacity of being proof against logic.

Having demonstrated that by this theory a forest may be considered as an organism, you think you have proved to the followers of the theory the incorrectness of their definition? Not at all. Their definition of an organism is so loose and plastic that they can apply it to everything they like.

Yes, they will say, you may consider the forest, too, as an organism. A forest is a mutual co-operation of the individuals who do not destroy each other; an aggregate: its parts can also pass into a closer relationship, and by differentiation and integration it may become an organism.

Then you will say, that in that case, the birds too and the insects, and the herbs of this forest, which mutually co-operate and do not destroy each other, may be considered, with the trees, to be an organism. They would agree to this, too. According to their theory, we may consider as an organism every collection of living beings which mutually co-operate, and do not destroy one another. You can establish a connection and co-operation between everything you like, and, according to evolution, you can assert that from anything may proceed anything else you like, if a long enough period is granted.

To those who believe in the Trinity, it is impossible to prove that it does not exist. But one can show them that their assertion is not based on knowledge, but is an assertion of faith, and that if they assert that there are three Gods, I have an equal right to assert that there are 17½ Gods. One may say the same thing with yet better ground to the followers of Positive and Evolutional science. On the basis of this science one could undertake to prove anything one liked. And the strangest thing of all is, that this same Positive science regards the scientific method as a condition of true knowledge, and that it has itself defined the elements of the scientific method. It professes that common sense is the scientific method. And yet common sense itself discloses the fallacies of the doctrine at every step. The moment those who occupied the position of saints felt there was no longer anything sacred in them, that they are cursed like the Pope and our own Synod, they immediately called themselves not merely sacred, but "most sacred." The moment science felt that it had given up common sense, it called itself The Science of Reason, The Only Really Scientific Science.

CHAPTER XXXI

"Division of Labour" is the law pervading everything that exists, therefore it must exist in human societies too. That may be so; but the question still remains, whether the existing division of labour in human society is the division which ought to exist. And when men consider a certain division of labour unreasonable and unjust, no science whatever can prove to men that what they consider unreasonable and unjust ought to continue.

The theological theory demonstrated that "Power is of God"; and it very well may be so. But the question still remains, To whom is the power given, to Catherine the Empress, or to the rebel Pugatchof? And no theological subtleties whatever can solve this difficulty. Moral philosophy demonstrates that "A State is merely a form of the social development of the individual"; but the question still remains,—Can the state of a Nero or that of a Gengis Khan be considered a form of such development? And no transcendentalism whatever can solve that difficulty.

It is the same with Scientific Science also. Division of Labour is the condition of the life of organisms and of human societies; but what have we to consider in these human societies as an organic division of labour? However much science studies the division of labour in the molecules of a tape-worm, all the observations cannot compel men to acknowledge as correct a division of labour which is repudiated by their reason and conscience. However convincing the proofs of the division of labour in the cells of investigated organisms may be, a man who has not yet lost his reason will say it is wrong that some should only weave cloth all their long life, and that this is not division of labour, but oppression of human beings.

Herbert Spencer and others affirm that as there is a whole population of weavers, the weaver's activity is in organic division of labour. In saying this they use a similar line of reasoning to the theologians: There is a power, therefore it is of God, whatever it may be: there are weavers, therefore they exist as a result of the law of division of labour. There might be some sense in this if the power and the position of weavers were created by themselves; but we know that they are not but that it is we who create them. Well, then, we ought to ascertain whether we have established this power according to the will of God or of ourselves, and whether we have called these weavers into being by virtue of some organic law or from some other cause.

Here are men earning their living by agriculture, as it is proper for all men to do: one man has set up a smith's forge and mended his plough; his neighbour comes to him and asks him to mend his plough, too, and promises to give labour or money in return. A second comes with a similar request; others follow; and in the society of these men a form of division of labour arises. Thus, one man becomes a smith.

Another man has taught his children well; his neighbour brings him his children and asks him to teach them, and thus a teacher is formed: but the smith as well as the teacher become, and continue to be, a smith and a teacher, only because they were asked, and they remain a smith and a teacher only as long as people require their trades. If it happens that too many smiths and teachers appear, or if their labour is no longer wanted, they at once, according to common sense, throw aside their trade and become labourers again, as it everywhere and always happens where there is no cause for the violation of a right division of labour.

Men who behave in such a way are directed both by their reason and their conscience; and therefore we who are endowed with reason and conscience, all agree that such a division of labour is a right one. But if it were to happen that smiths, having the possibility of compelling other men to labour for them, were to continue to make horseshoes when there was no longer a demand for them, and teachers were to wish to continue to teach when there was nobody to be taught, then, to every impartial man endowed with reason and conscience, it would be obvious that this is not real division of labour but a usurpation of other men's labour; because such a division could no longer be tested satisfactorily by the sole standard by which we may know whether it is right or not,—the demand of such labour by other men, and a voluntary compensation offered for it by them. But exactly such a surplus, however, is what Scientific Science terms "a division of labour."

Men do what is not required, and they ask to be fed for it, and say it is just, because it is division of labour. The chief *social* evil of a people,—not with us alone,—is the countless horde of State officials. The chief cause of the *economical* misery of our days, is what is called in England "over-production" (that is, the production of an enormous quantity of articles, wanted by nobody, and which no one knows how to get rid of). All this comes simply from the strange idea about the "division of labour?"

It would be very strange to see a boot-maker who considered that men were bound to feed him because, forsooth, he continued to produce boots wanted by no one; but what shall we say about those men in government, church, science, and art, who not only do not produce any thing tangibly useful for the people but whose produce is wanted by nobody, yet who as boldly require to be well fed and clothed on account of "The division of labour."

There may be magicians for whose activity there is a demand and to whom men give casks and spirits; but we cannot even imagine the existence of magicians who, while their magic is not wanted by anybody, require to be fed simply because they wish to practice their art. Yet in our world this is the very position of the men in church and state, of the men of science and art. And it all proceeds from that false conception of the division of labour, defined, not by reason and conscience, but by deductions to which these scientists so unanimously resort.

Division of labour, indeed, has always existed; but it is correct only when man decides it by his reason and conscience, and not by his making observations on it. And the conscience and the reason of all men solve this question in the simplest and surest way. They always decide the question by recognizing the division of labour to be right only when the special activity of a man is so necessary to others, that they freely offer to feed him in compensation for what they ask him to do for them. But when a man from his infancy up to his thirtieth year lives on the shoulders of other men, promising to do, when he finishes his studies, something very useful, which nobody has ever asked him for, and then for the rest of his life lives in the same way, promising only to do presently something which nobody asks him to do, this would not be a true division of labour, but, as it really is, only the violation by a strong man of the labour of others; the same appropriation of other men's labour by a strong man, which formerly Theology called Divine predestination; Philosophy, Inevitable Conditions of Life; and now Scientific Science, the Organic Division of Labour.

The entire importance of the ruling science consists in this alone. This science is now the dispenser of diplomas for idleness, because in her temples she alone analyzes and determines what activity in the social organism is parasitic and what organic. As if each man could not decide much better and more quickly, too, by consulting his own reason and conscience.

As formerly, both for clergy and for statesmen, there could have been no doubt as to who were most necessary to other people, so now for the believers in Positive Science it seems that there can be no doubt about this, that their own activity is undoubtedly an organic one: they, the factors of science and art, are the cells of the brain, the most precious cells of all the human organism.

Let us leave them to reign, eat, drink, and be feasted, as priests and sophists of old have before them, so long as they do not deprave men!

Since men are reasonable creatures they have discriminated good from evil, making use of what has been done in this direction before them by others, have struggled with evil, seeking a true and better way, and slowly but unceasingly have advanced in this way. But always across the road different deceptions stood before them, trying to assure them that this struggle was not at all necessary, and that they should submit to the tide of life. First the awful deceptions of the old Church; little by little with dreadful struggle and effort men got rid of them: but scarcely had they done so when in their place arose new ones—state and philosophical deceptions.

Men freed themselves from these too, and now a new deceit, a still worse one, has sprung up in their path,—the scientific deception.

This new deception is exactly what the old ones were: its essence consists in the substitution of an externality for reason and conscience, and this externality is *observation*, as in theology it was *revelation*.

The snare of this science consists in this, that having exposed some bare-faced perversions of the activity of reason and conscience, it destroys men's confidence in both reason and conscience. Hiding their lie clothed in a scientific theory, scientists assure men that by studying external phenomena they study undeniable facts which will reveal to them the law of man's life. Things which are the property of conscience and reason are now to be discovered by observation alone. These men lose the conception of good and evil and thus become unable to understand those expressions and definitions of good and evil which have been worked out during the entire former existence of mankind.

All that reason and conscience say to them, all that they have said to the highest representatives of men since the world has existed, all this, in their slang, is "conditional and subjective." All this must be left behind.

It is said that by reason one cannot apprehend the truth, because reason is liable to error: there is another way, unmistakable and almost mechanical,—one must study facts on the ground of science; that is, on two groundless suppositions, Positivism and Evolution, which are offered as the most undoubted truths. With mock solemnity the ruling science asserts that the solution of all the questions of life is only possible through studying the facts of nature, and especially those of organisms.

The credulous crowd of youth, overwhelmed by the novelty of this authority,—not only not destroyed, not yet even touched by critics,—rush to the study of these facts of natural sciences, to that "only way" which, according to the assertion of the ruling doctrine, alone can lead to the elucidation of all questions of life. But the farther the students proceed in this study, the farther do they remove not only the possibility of solving the questions of life, but even the very thought of this solution. The more they grow accustomed, not so much to observe themselves, as to believe other men's observations on their word (to believe in cells, in protoplasm, in the fourth dimension of matter, and so on), the more the form hides from them the contents. The more they lose the consciousness of good and evil and the capacity of understanding those expressions and definitions of good and evil which have been worked out in all the former career of mankind, the more they appropriate to themselves that special scientific slang of "conditional" expressions which have no common human meaning in them. The farther and farther they get into the thick forest of observations lighted by anything, the more they lose the capacity, not only of independent thought, but even of understanding other men's fresh human ideas which are not included in their Talmud. But chiefly they pass their best years in losing the habit of life, that is, of labour, and accustom themselves to consider their own position justified, and thus become, physically, good-for-nothing parasites, and, mentally, dislocate their brains and lose all power of thought-production.

So, their capacities more and more blunted, they acquire by degrees self-assurance which deprives them forever of the possibility of returning to a simple, laborious life, and to any plain, clear, common, human manner of thinking.

CHAPTER XXXII

The division of labour has always existed in human society, and I daresay always will exist; but the question for us is, not if it has been and will still continue, but, what should guide us in providing that this division may be a right one.

If we take the facts of observation for our standard, we refuse to have any standard at all: for every division of labour which we see among men, and which may seem to us to be right, we shall consider right; and this is what the ruling Scientific Science is leading us to.

Division of labour!

"Some are occupied with mental and spiritual, others with muscular and physical, labour."

With what an assurance men express this! They wish to think it, and so that which is transparently the ancient violence, seems to them in reality a fair exchange of services.

"Thou," or rather, "you" (because it is always the many who have to feed the one),— "you feed me, dress me, do for me all this rough labour which I require of you, and to which you are accustomed from your infancy, and I will do for you that mental work to which I have already become accustomed. Give me bodily food, and in return I will give you the spiritual."

The statement seems fair; and it would really be so if such exchange of services were free; if those who supply the bodily food were not obliged to supply it before they get the spiritual. The producer of the spiritual food says, "In order that I may be able to give you this food, you must feed me, clothe me, and remove all filth from my house."

But the producer of bodily food must do his work without making any claims of his own, and he has to give the bodily food whether he receive spiritual food or not. If the exchange were a free one the conditions on both sides would be equal. We agree that spiritual food is as necessary to man as bodily. But the learned man, the artist, says, "Before we can begin to serve men by giving them spiritual food, we want men to provide us with bodily food."

But why should not the producers of this say, "Before we begin to serve you with bodily food, we want spiritual food; and until we receive it, we cannot labour?"

You say, "I require the labour of a ploughman, a smith, a book-maker, a carpenter, masons, and others, in order that I may prepare the spiritual food I have to offer."

Every workman might say, too, "Before I go to work to prepare bodily food for you, I want the fruits of the spirit. In order to have strength for labouring, I require a religious teaching, the social order of common life, application of knowledge to labour, and the joys and comforts which art gives. I have no time to work out for myself a teaching concerning the meaning of life,—give it to me. I have no time to think out statutes of common life which would prevent the violation of justice,—give me this too. I have no time to study mechanics, natural philosophy, chemistry, technology; give me books with information as to how I am to improve my tools, my ways of working, my dwelling, its heating and lighting. I have no time to occupy myself with poetry, with plastic art, or music. Give me the excitements and comforts necessary for life; give me the productions of the arts."

You say it would be impossible for you to do your important and necessary business if you were deprived of the labour that working-people do for you; and I say, a workman may declare, "It is impossible for me to do my important and necessary business, not less important than yours,—to plough, to cart away refuse, and to clean *your* houses,—if I am deprived of a religious guidance corresponding to the wants of my intellect and my conscience, of a reasonable government which will secure my labour, of information for easing my labour, and the enjoyment of art to ennoble it. All you have hitherto offered me in the shape of spiritual food is not only of no use to me whatever, I cannot even understand to whom it could be of any use. And until I receive this nourishment, proper for me as for every man, I cannot produce bodily food to feed you with."

What if the working-people should speak thus? And if they did, it would be no jest but the simplest justice. If a workman said this, he would be far more in the right than a man of intellectual labour; because the labour produced by the workman is more urgent and more necessary than that of the intellectual worker, and because a man of intellect is hindered by nothing from giving that spiritual food which he promised to give, while the workingman is hindered in giving the bodily food by the fact that he himself is short of it.

What, then, should we intellectual labourers answer, if such simple and lawful claims were made upon us? How should we satisfy these claims? Should we satisfy the religious wants of the people by the catechism of Philaret, by sacred histories of

Sokolof, by the literature sent out by monasteries and cathedrals? Should we satisfy their demand for order by the "Code of Laws," and cassation verdicts of different departments, or by reports of committees and commissions? And should we satisfy their want of knowledge by giving them spectrum analysis, a survey of the Milky Way, speculative geometry, microscopic investigations, controversies concerning spiritualism and mediumism, the activity of academies of science? How should we satisfy their artistic wants? By Pushkin, Dostoyevsky, Turgenief, L. Tolstoy? By pictures of French *salons*, and of those of our artists who represent naked women, satin, velvet, and landscapes, and pictures of domestic life; by the music of Wagner, and that of our own musicians?

All this is of no use and cannot be of use because we, with our right to utilize the labour of the people and absence of all duties in preparation of their spiritual food, have quite lost from sight the single destination our activity should have.

We do not even know what is required by the workman; we have even forgotten his mode of life, his views of things, his language; we have even lost sight of the very working-people themselves, and we study them like some ethnographical rarity or newly-discovered continent. Demanding for ourselves bodily food, we have taken upon ourselves to provide the spiritual; but in consequence of the imaginary division of labour, according to which we may not only first take our dinner and afterwards do our work, but may during many generations dine luxuriously and do no work,—we, in the way of compensation for our food, have prepared something which is of use, as it seems to us, for ourselves and for science and art, but of no use whatever for those very people whose labour we consume under the pretext of providing them in return with intellectual food; not only is of no use, but is quite unintelligible and distasteful to them.

In our blindness, we have to such a degree left out of sight the duty we took upon us, that we have even forgotten for what our labour is being done; and the very people whom we undertook to serve we have made an object of our scientific and artistic activities. We study them and represent them for our own pleasure and amusement: but we have quite forgotten that it is our duty, not to study and depict, but to serve them.

We have to such a degree left out of sight the duty we assumed that we have not even noticed that other people do what we undertook in the departments of science and art, and that our place turns out to be occupied.

It appears that while we have been in controversy,—now about the immaculate conception, and now about spontaneous generation; now about spiritualism, and now about the forms of atoms; now about pangenesis, now about protoplasms, and so on,—all this while the people none the less required spiritual food, and the abortive outcasts of science and art began to provide for the people this spiritual food to the order of various speculators, who had in view exclusively their own profit and gain.

Now, for some forty years in Europe, and ten years in Russia, millions of books and pictures and songs have been circulating; shows have been opened: and the people gaze and sing, and receive intellectual food, though not from those who promised to provide it for them; and we, who justify our idleness by the need for that intellectual food which we pretend to provide for the people, are sitting still, and taking no notice.

But we cannot do so, because our final justification has vanished from under our feet. We have taken upon ourselves a peculiar department: we have a peculiar functional activity of our own. We are the brain of the people. They feed us, and we have undertaken to teach them. Only for the sake of this have we freed ourselves from labour. What, then, have we been teaching them? They have waited years, tens of years, hundreds of years. And we are still conversing among ourselves, and teaching each other, and amusing ourselves, and have quite forgotten them; we have so totally forgotten them, that others have taken upon themselves to teach and amuse them, and we have not even become aware of this in our flippant talk about division of labour: and it is very obvious that all our talk about the utility we offer to the people was only a shameful excuse.

CHAPTER XXXIII

There was a time when the *Church* guided the intellectual life of the men of our world. The Church promised men happiness, and, in compensation for this she freed herself from taking part in mankind's common struggle for life.

As soon as she did this she went away from her calling, and men turned from her. It was not the *errors* of the Church which originally caused her ruin, but the fact that by the help of the secular power, in the time of Constantine, her ministers violated the law of labour; and then their claim to idleness and luxury gave birth to the errors.

As soon as she obtained this power she began to care for herself, and not for humanity, whom she had taken upon herself to serve. The ministers of the Church gave themselves up to idleness and depravity.

The State took upon itself to guide men's lives. The State promised men justice, peace, security, order, satisfaction of common intellectual and material wants; and, in compensation, men who served the State freed themselves from taking part in the struggle for life. And the State's servants, as soon as they were able to utilize other men's labour, acted in the same way as the ministers of the Church.

They had not in view the people; but, from kings down to the lowest state functionaries, in Rome, as well as in France, England, Russia, and America, they gave themselves over to idleness and depravity. Now men have lost their faith in the state, and anarchy is now seriously advocated as an ideal. The state has lost its prestige among men, only because its ministers have claimed the right of utilizing the people's labour for themselves.

Science and art have done the same, assisted by the state power which they took upon themselves to sustain. They also have claimed and obtained for themselves the right of idleness and of utilizing other men's labour, and also have been false to their calling. And their errors, too, proceeded only from the fact that their ministers, pointing to a falsely conceived principle of the division of labour, claimed for themselves the right to utilize the work of the people, and so lost the meaning of their calling, making the aim of their activity, not the utility of the people, but some mysterious activity of science and art; and also, like their forerunners, they have given themselves over to idleness and depravity, though not so much to a fleshly as to an intellectual corruption.

It is said that science and art have done much for mankind.

That is quite true.

Church and State have given much to humanity, not because they abused their power, or because their ministers forsook the common life of men, and the eternal duty of labour for life—but in spite of this.

The Roman Republic was powerful, not because its citizens were able to lead a life of depravity, but because it could number among them men who were virtuous.

This is the case with science and art.

Science and art have effected much for mankind, not because their ministers had sometimes formerly, and have always at present, the possibility of freeing themselves from labour, but because men of genius, not utilizing these rights, have forwarded the progress of mankind.

The class of learned men and artists who claim, on account of a false division of labour, the right of utilizing other men's labour, cannot contribute to the progress of true science and true art, because a lie can never produce a truth.

We are so accustomed to our pampered or debilitated representatives of intellectual labour, that it would seem very strange if a learned man or an artist were to plough, or cart manure. We think that, were he to do so, all would go to ruin; that all his wisdom would be shaken out of him, and that the great artistic images he carries in his breast would be soiled by the manure: but we are so accustomed to our present conditions that we do not wonder at our ministers of science, that is, ministers and teachers of truth, compelling other people to do for them that which they could very well do themselves, passing half their time eating, smoking, chattering in "liberal" gossip, reading newspapers, novels, visiting theatres; we are not surprised to see our philosopher in an inn, in a theatre, at a ball; we do not wonder when we learn that those artists who delight and ennoble our souls, pass their lives in drunkenness, in playing cards, in company with loose women, or do things still worse.

Science and art are fine things: but just because they are fine things men ought not to spoil them by associating them with depravity;—by freeing themselves from man's duty to serve by labour his own life and the lives of other men.

Science and art have forwarded the progress of mankind. Yes; but not because men of science and art, under the pretext of a division of labour, taught men by word, and chiefly by deed, to utilize by violence the misery and sufferings of the people in order to free themselves from the very first and unquestionable human duty of labouring with their hands in the common struggle of mankind with nature.

CHAPTER XXXIV

"But," you say, "it is this very division of labour, the freeing men of science and of art from the necessity of earning their bread, that has rendered possible the extraordinary success in science which we see to-day.

"If everybody were to plough, these enormous results would not be attained; you would not have those astonishing successes which have so enlarged man's power over nature; you would not have those discoveries in astronomy which so strike the minds of men and promote navigation; there would be no steamers, railways, wonderful bridges, tunnels, steam-engines, telegraphs, photographs, telephones, sewing-machines, phonographs, electricity, telescopes, spectroscopes, microscopes, chloroform, Lister bandages, carbolic acid."

I will not attempt to enumerate all the things of which our century is proud. This enumeration, and the ecstasy of the contemplation of ourselves and of our great deeds you can find in almost every newspaper and popular book. And these raptures are so often repeated, and we are so seldom tired of praising ourselves, that we really have come to believe, with Jules Verne, that science and art never made such progress as in our time. And as all this is rendered possible only by division of labour, how can we avoid countenancing it?

Let us suppose that the progress of our century is really striking, astonishing, extraordinary; let us suppose, too, that we are particularly lucky in living at such an extraordinary time: but let us try to ascertain the value of these successes, not by our own self-contentment, but by the very principle of the division of labour; that is, by the intellectual labour of scientists for the advantage of the people which has to compensate for the freedom of its servants from manual toil.

This progress is very striking indeed; but owing to some bad luck, recognized, too, by the men of science, this progress has not yet ameliorated, but has rather deteriorated, the condition of working men.

Though a working man, instead of walking, can use the railway, it is this very railway which has caused his forest to be burned and has carried away his bread from under his very nose, and put him into a condition which is next door to slavery to the railway proprietor.

If, thanks to steam-engines and machines, a workman can buy cheap and bad calico, it is these very engines and machines which have deprived him of his livelihood and brought him to a state of entire slavery to the manufacturer.

If there are telegraphs, which he is not forbidden to use but which he does not use because he cannot afford it, still each of his productions, the value of which rises, is bought up at low prices before his very eyes by capitalists, thanks to that telegraph, before he has even become aware that the article is in demand.

If there are telephones and telescopes, novels, operas, picture-galleries, and so on, the life of the workman is not at all improved by any of them, because all, owing to the same unlucky chance, are beyond his reach.

So that, after all, these wonderful discoveries and productions of art, if they have not made the life of working-people worse, have by no means improved it: and on this the men of science are agreed.

So that, if we apply, not our self-contemplating rapture, but the very standard on which the ground of the division of labour is defended,—utility to the working-world,—to the question as to the reality of the successes attained by the sciences and arts, we shall see that we have not yet any sound reason for the self-contentment to which we consign ourselves so willingly.

A peasant uses the railway; a peasant's wife buys calico; in the cottage a lamp, and not a pine-knot, burns; and the peasant lights his pipe with a match,—all this is comfortable; but what right have I from this to say that railways and factories have done good to the people?

If a peasant uses the railway, and buys a lamp, calico, and matches, he does it only because we cannot forbid his doing so: but we all know very well that railways and factories were not built for the use of the people; and why, then, should the casual comfort a workman obtains by chance be brought forward as a proof of the usefulness of these institutions to the people?

We all know very well that if the engineers and capitalists who build a railway or a factory thought about the working-people, they thought only how to make the most possible use of them. And we see they have fully succeeded in doing so in Europe and America, as well as in Russia.

In every hurtful thing there is something useful. After a house has been burned down we can sit and warm ourselves, and light our pipes from one of the fire-brands; but should we therefore say that a conflagration is beneficial?

Whatever we do, do not let us deceive ourselves. We all know very well the motives for building railways and factories, and for producing kerosene and matches. An engineer builds a railway for the government, to facilitate wars, or for the capitalists for their financial purposes. He makes machines for manufacturers for his own advantage and for the profit of capitalists. All that he makes or plans he does for the purpose of the government, the capitalists, and other rich people. His most skilful inventions are either directly harmful to the people, such as guns, torpedoes, solitary prisons, and so on; or they are not only useless but quite inaccessible to them, such as electric light, telephones, and the innumerable improvements of comfort; or lastly, they deprave the people and rob them of their last kopek, that is, their last labour, for spirits, wine, beer, opium, tobacco, finery, and all sorts of trifles.

But if it happens sometimes that the inventions of men of science and the works of engineers, are of use to the people, as, for instance, railways, calicoes, steel, scythes, it only proves that in this world of ours everything is mutually connected, and that out of every hurtful activity there may arise an accidental good for those to whom the activity was hurtful.

Men of science and of art could say that their activity was useful for the people, only if in their activity they have aimed at serving the people, as they now aim to serve the government and capitalists.

We could have said that, only if the men of science and art made the wants of the people their object; but such is not the case.

All learned men are occupied with their sacred businesses, which lead to the investigation of protoplasms, the spectrum analysis of stars, and so on: but concerning investigations as to how to set an axe, or with what kind it is more advantageous to hew; which saw is the most handy; with what flour bread shall be made, how it may best be kneaded, how to set it to rise; how to heat and to build stoves; what food, drink or crockery-ware it is best to use; what mushrooms may be eaten, and how they may be prepared more conveniently,—science never troubles itself, or does so very slightly.

Yet all this is the business of science.

I know that, according to its own definition, science must be useless; but this is only an excuse, and a very impudent one.

The business of science is to serve people. We have invented telegraphs, telephones, phonographs, but what improvements have we made in the life of the people? We have catalogued two millions of insects! but have we domesticated a single animal since biblical times, when all our animals had long been domesticated, and still the elk and the deer, and the partridge and the grouse and the wood-hen, are wild?

Botanists have discovered the cells, and in the cells protoplasms and in protoplasms something else, and in this something else again.

These occupations will go on for a long time and evidently never end, and therefore learned men have no time to do anything useful. Hence from the times of the ancient Egyptians and Hebrews, when wheat and lentils were already cultivated, down to the present time, not a single plant has been added for the nourishment of the people except potatoes, and these were not discovered by science. We have invented torpedoes and house-drains; but the spinning-wheel, weaving-looms, ploughs and axe-handles, flails and rakes, buckets and well-sweeps, are still the same as in the time of Rurik. If some things have been improved, it is not the learned who have improved them, but the unlearned.

The same is the case with art. Many people are acclaimed as great writers. We have carefully analyzed their works, have written mountains of critiques and criticisms upon criticisms, and still more criticisms on criticisms; we have collected pictures in galleries, and thoroughly studied in detail different schools of art; and we possess symphonies and operas that it is with great difficulty we ourselves can listen to; but what have we added to the folk-lore, legends, tales, songs for the people? what pictures, what music, have we created for the people?

Books and pictures are published, and harmoniums are made for the people, but we did not participate in either.

What is most striking and obvious is the false tendency of our science and art, which manifests itself in those departments which, according to their own propositions, would seem to be useful to people, but which, owing to this tendency, appear rather pernicious than useful. An engineer, a surgeon, a teacher, an artist, an author, seem by their very professions to be obliged to serve the people, but what do we see? With the present tendency, they can bring to the people nothing but harm. An engineer and a mechanic must work with capital: without capital they are good for nothing.

All their training is of such a nature that, in order to make use of it, they need capital and the employment of work-people on a large scale, to say nothing of the fact that they themselves are accustomed to spend from fifteen hundred to a thousand rubles a year on themselves, and therefore cannot go to live in a village, since no one there can give them any such remuneration: from their very occupations they are not fit for the service of the people.

They understand how to calculate the arch of a bridge by means of the higher mathematics, how to calculate power and the transfer of power in an engine, and so on: but they are at a loss to meet the plain requirements of common labour; they do not know how to improve the plough or the cart; or how to make a brook passable, taking into consideration the conditions of a workman's life.

They know and understand nothing of all this, less even than the poorest peasant does. Give them workshops, and plenty of people, order engines from abroad, and then they will arrange these matters. But to find out how to ease the labour of the millions of the people in their present conditions, they do not know, and cannot do it; and therefore, by their knowledge and habits and wants, they are not at all fit for this business.

A surgeon is in a still worse condition. His imaginary science is of such a nature that he understands how to cure those only who have nothing to do and who can utilize other men's labour. He requires a countless number of expensive accessories, instruments, medicines, sanitary dwellings, food, and drains, in order that he may act scientifically: besides his fee he demands such expenses that, in order to cure one patient, he must kill with starvation hundreds of those who bear this expense.

He has studied under eminent persons in the capital cities, who attended only to those patients whom they may take into hospitals, or who can afford to buy all the necessary medicines and machines, and even go at once from north to south, to these or those mineral waters, as the case may be.

Their science is of such a kind that every country surgeon complains that there is no possibility of attending to the work-people who are so poor that they cannot afford sanitary accommodations, and that there are no hospitals, and that he cannot attend to the business alone, that he requires help and assistant-surgeons.

What does this really mean?

It means this,—that the want of the necessaries of life is the chief cause of people's misfortunes, and the source of diseases as well as of their spreading and incurability. Now science, under the banner of "the division of labour," calls its champions to help the people. Science has settled satisfactorily about the rich classes, and seeks how to cure those who can get everything necessary for the purpose; and it sends persons to cure in the same way those who have nothing to spare. But there are no means; and therefore they must be raised from the people, who become ill and catch diseases, and cannot be cured for want of means.

The advocates of the healing art for the people say, that, up to the present time, this business has not been sufficiently developed.

Evidently it is not yet developed, because if (which God forbid!) it were developed among our people, and, instead of two doctors and mid-wives and two assistant-surgeons in the district, there should be twenty sent, as they want, then there would soon be no one left to attend to. The scientific co-operation for the benefit of the people must be of quite a different kind. And this, which ought to exist, has not yet begun.

It will begin when a man of science, an engineer, or a surgeon, ceases to consider lawful that division of labour, or rather that taking away other men's labour, which now exists, and when he no longer considers that he has the right to take,—I do not say hundreds of thousands,—but even a moderate sum of one thousand or five hundred rubles as compensation for his services; but when such a man comes to live among labouring-people in the same condition and in the same way as they, and applies his information in mechanics, technics or hygiene, to cure them.

But at present, scientific men, who are fed at the expense of the workman, have quite forgotten the conditions of the life of these men: they ignore (as they say) these conditions, and are quite seriously offended that their imaginary knowledge does not find application among the people.

The departments of the healing art as well as of the mechanical have not yet been touched: the questions how best to divide the period of labour, how and upon what it is best to feed, how best to dress, how to counteract dampness and cold, how best to wash, to suckle, and swaddle children, and so on, and all these applied to the conditions in which the workers now exist,—all these questions have not yet been faced.

The same applies to the activity of scientific teachers,—the pedagogues. Science has arranged this business, too, in such a way, that teaching according to science is possible only for those who are rich; and the teachers, like the engineers and surgeons, are involuntarily drawn towards money, and among us in Russia especially towards the government.

And this cannot be otherwise, because a school properly arranged (and the general rule is that the more scientifically a school is arranged the more expensive it is), with convertible benches, globes, maps, libraries, and manuals for teachers and pupils, is just such a school to maintain which it is necessary to double the taxes of the people. So science wants to have it. The children are necessary for work, and the more so with the poorer people. The advocates of science say, "Pedagogy is even now of use for the people; but let it develop, then it will be still better." But if it will develop till instead of 20 schools in a district there will be 100—all of them scientific,—and the parents forced to keep up these schools? Then they will be still poorer, and will want the labour of their children still more urgently.

What is to be done then?

To this they will reply, "The government will establish schools, and will make education obligatory as it is in the rest of Europe." But the money will still have to be raised from the people, and labour will be still harder for them, and they will have less time to spare from their labour, and there will then be no obligatory education at all.

There is, again, only one escape,—for a teacher to live in the conditions of a workman, and to teach for that compensation which will be freely offered him.

Such is the false tendency of science which deprives it of the possibility to fulfil its duty in serving the people. But this false tendency of our educated class is still more obvious in art-activity, which, for the sake of its very meaning ought to be accessible to the people.

Science may point to its stupid excuse that "science is acting for science," and that, when fully developed it will become accessible to the people; but art, if it is art indeed, ought to be accessible to all, especially to those for whose sake it is created. But our art strikingly denounces its factors in that they do not wish, and do not understand, and are not able to be of use to the people. A painter, in order to produce his great works, must have a large studio, in which at least forty joiners or boot-makers might work, who are now freezing or suffocating in wretched lodgings. But this is not all: he requires models, costumes, journeys from place to place. The Academy of Art has spent millions of rubles, collected from the people, for the encouragement of art; and the productions of this art are hung in palaces, and are neither intelligible to the people nor wanted by them.

Musicians, in order to express their great ideas, must gather about two hundred men with white neckties or in special costumes, and spend hundreds of thousands of rubles arranging operas. But this art-production would never appear to the people (even if they could afford to use it) as anything but perplexing or dull.

The authors, writers, would seem not to need any particular accommodations, studios, models, orchestras, or actors; but here also it turns out that an author, a writer, in order to prepare his great works, wants travelling, palaces, cabinets, enjoyments of art, theatres, concerts, mineral waters, and so on; to say nothing of all the comforts of his dwelling and all the comforts of his life. If he himself has not saved up enough money for this purpose he is given a pension in order that he may compose better. And, again, these writings, which we value so highly, remain for the people, rubbish, and are not at all necessary to them.

What if, according to the wish of men of science and art, such producers of mental food should so multiply, that, in every village it would be necessary to build a studio, provide an orchestra, and keep an author in the conditions which men of art consider indispensable to them? I dare say working-people would make a vow never to look at a picture, or listen to a symphony, or read poetry and novels, in order only not to be compelled to feed all these good-for-nothing parasites.

And why should not men of art serve the people? In every cottage there are holy images and pictures; each peasant, each woman of the people, sings; many have instruments of music; and all can relate stories, repeat poetry; and many of them read. How came it to pass that these two things, which were as much made for one another as a key for a lock, were separated, and why are they so separated that we cannot imagine how to re-unite them?

Tell a painter to paint without a studio, models, costumes, and to draw penny pictures, and he will say that this would be a denial of art as he understands it. Tell a musician to play on a harmonium and to teach country-women to sing songs; tell a poet to throw aside writing poems and novels and satires, and to compose song-books for the people, and stories and tales which might be intelligible to illiterate persons,—they will say you are cracked.

But is it not being worse than cracked when the men who have freed themselves from labour because they promised to provide mental food for those who have brought them up, and are feeding and clothing them, have afterwards so forgotten their promise that they have ceased to understand how to make food fit for the people? Yet this very forsaking of their promises they consider dignifies them.

Such is the case everywhere, they say. Then everywhere the case is very unreasonable. And it will be so while men, under the pretext of division of labour, promise to provide mental food for the people, but only swallow up the labour of the people. Men will serve the people with science and art only when living among them and in the same way as the people do, putting forth no claims whatever, they offer to the people their scientific and artistic services, leaving it to the free will of the people to accept or refuse them.

Printed by Libri Plureos GmbH in Hamburg,
Germany